BAKING BASICS

and BEYOND

PAT SINCLAIR

SURREY BOOKS
CHICAGO

Surrey Books is an imprint of Agate Publishing, Inc.
Edited by Bookcrafters, Inc., Chicago
Designed and typeset by Joan Sommers Design, Chicago
Printed in the United States.

Library of Congress Cataloging-in-Publication Data

Sinclair, Patricia.
  Baking basics and beyond / by Pat Sinclair.
     p. cm.
  Includes index.
  ISBN-13: 978-1-57284-082-9 (pbk.)
  ISBN-10: 1-57284-082-X (pbk.)
  1. Baking. I. Title.

TX763.S535 2006
641.8'15—dc22

                           2006022204

10 9 8 7 6 5 4 3 2 1

Agate books are available in bulk at discount prices. For more information, go to agatepublishing.com.

table of contents

acknowledgments

SEVERAL YEARS AGO I realized that I had gained considerable knowledge about baking and that I enjoyed sharing that knowledge. This book is the result. As I wrote these recipes, I realized how much influence my mother had on my baking skills and on my childhood memories of baking.

I wish to thank my husband, Duncan, for always being my best friend and encouraging me throughout my career. Thanks also to my children, who supported me by testing lots of recipes and giving me detailed feedback and editing.

Susan Schwartz, my publisher, gave me the opportunity to publish this, my first book, and Doug Seibold finished the project. Dianne Jacob helped me write my proposal and was generous with her advice. My friends and recipe-testers made all the difference with their unending support. I thank them all.

introduction

· ·

ANYONE WHO HAS TASTED a tender flaky biscuit hot out of the oven, melting in their mouth, knows that homemade biscuits are very different from biscuits made with refrigerated dough. Brownies baked from a mix are chocolaty and moist, but homemade Fabulous Fudgy Brownies (see page 72) have an incomparable chocolate flavor and dense texture and are topped with a smooth, buttery, chocolate glaze. As you use this book, you'll find many reasons why home baking is best.

Successful baking depends on following the directions of a carefully crafted recipe. Pay attention to details because most baked goods are the result of the chemical inter-actions of simple ingredients. Read the entire recipe before you begin preparation. This way you will have all the ingredients ready and not have to stop in the middle to find a missing ingredient or pan. Chefs set out all their ingredients and equipment before beginning, and such organization encourages success.

Read the introduction to each chapter to learn about specific ingredients and techniques for the baked goods featured. To me, one of the most exciting things about baking is the interconnection among techniques. After you learn how to cut shortening into flour for making biscuits, you will also know how to make a flaky streusel topping for a coffee cake.

equipment

Any book on basic baking must include a list of the basic equipment needed to get started. As your baking skills advance, you will probably want to purchase additional items such as specialty baking pans. In any event, buy good-quality equipment, and it will last for many years.

To begin, you need an electric mixer and assorted sizes of bowls. A heavy-duty mixer makes everything easy, but hand-held mixers also work. You also need measuring cups, separate sets to measure liquid and dry ingredients, as the cups are not interchangeable. It's good to have more than one clear glass or clear plastic measuring cup for liquids so you don't have to stop and wash the cup in the middle of a recipe. Buy at least two 1-cup glass measuring cups, two 2-cup measuring cups, and one 4-cup measuring cup.

A complete set of dry measuring cups includes ¼, ⅓, ½, and 1-cup measures. A complete set of measuring spoons includes ¼, ½, 1 teaspoon, and 1 tablespoon spoons. It is convenient to have a second set but not necessary. (See How to Measure, page 13.)

An attractive ceramic crock is a useful way to corral utensils and keeps them handy on the counter. Buy at least two rubber spatulas and two sizes of wire whisks (small and medium). Large spoons and inset metal spatulas have many uses. A microplane grater is the easiest way to grate citrus peel, and I think it is my most useful utensil. Don't forget a pastry brush, ruler, and scissors. Silicone pastry brushes are great because they can be washed in the dishwasher.

A sifter thoroughly mixes dry ingredients, and sifting adds air pockets that expand and aid the dough to rise during baking. A wire mesh strainer can be used as a sifter, if you prefer.

A pastry blender (or dough blender) is used to blend fat with flour, creating many flaky layers in pastries. Also, be sure you have a rolling pin, biscuit- and cookie-cutters, and a pizza wheel. (I use a pizza wheel a lot!)

For the best baking results, check the oven temperature with an oven thermometer, and adjust your oven settings if necessary. An instant-read thermometer helps prevent overcooking custard sauces and measures the heat of liquids when baking yeast breads. Test your instant-read thermometer by placing it in boiling water— it should read 212°F. Use this as a guideline to make any adjustments.

There are many sizes of pans used in baking. As a beginning baker, you do not need every kind. As you continue baking, though, you'll probably decide to purchase more pans based on your own needs. For evenly browned results, use high-quality aluminum pans. If your pans are dark with a nonstick coating, reduce the oven temperature or take a peek before the baking time is up. Pans with nonstick coating need to be washed by hand. For the most basic pan selection you'll need:

Two 8- or 9-inch round cake pans with straight sides
One 8- or 9-inch square pan
One 9-inch springform pan
One tube pan with removable bottom
One nonstick fluted tube pan
One 9-inch tart pan with removable bottom
One 13 x 9-inch baking pan
Two 9 x 5-inch loaf pans
One 9-inch metal pie pan or glass pie plate
Two (at least) cookie sheets
One jellyroll pan (15 x 10 x 1 inch)
Six 6-ounce custard cups
Muffin pans in several sizes
Two wire cooling racks

INGREDIENTS

If you understand the interaction of the ingredients used for baking, you will be a better baker. Once you know about the different types of flours and the differences between butter and shortening and the properties of the many ingredients, you will see how they affect the final baked product.

FLOUR

Almost every baked product contains flour. Flour provides the structure for baked goods because the proteins in flour combine with the liquid ingredients to make gluten. The amount of gluten formed relates to the tenderness of the end product. In cakes, just a little gluten is the key, whereas in yeast breads more gluten is needed to support the sturdy texture of the bread. The different types of flour are the result of blending different kinds of wheat during milling. In this book several kinds of flour are used: all-purpose, bread, whole wheat, and cake flour.

All-purpose flour contains enough protein to provide structure for yeast breads while it also can be used for cakes and pastries. Flour bleaches naturally, but some flour is bleached chemically, thus altering the protein. Bleached flour is lighter in color than unbleached. Bleached flour often is preferred for tender pie crusts and cookies.

Bread flour is milled from hard winter wheat and contains the highest amount of protein, so it creates breads with greater volume. Dough made with bread flour requires more kneading because of the high amount of protein in the flour.

Whole wheat flour is ground from the entire wheat kernel and has more fiber and higher nutritional value than other types of flour. Because it contains the germ of the wheat kernel, which contains fat, it can become rancid. To lengthen the shelf life of whole wheat flour, store it in the freezer. Do not completely substitute whole wheat flour for all-purpose or bread flour in recipes or the baked goods will be very heavy and dense. Replace no more than half of the all-purpose or bread flour with whole wheat flour.

Cake flour contains the least amount of protein but is perfect for light, tender cakes.

Self-rising flour has baking powder and salt added during milling. If you bake a lot of biscuits, muffins, or quick breads, it is convenient to have this on hand. One cup contains 1½ teaspoons of baking powder and ½ teaspoon of salt.

EGGS

Eggs provide structure, richness, browning, and tenderness in baking. All of my recipes were developed using large eggs. Eggs must be stored in the refrigerator and are easier to separate when cold. Since egg whites reach their highest volume when they are beaten at room temperature, allow them to stand at room temperature about 30 minutes before beating.

It's better not to bake a meringue-topped pie on a humid day because meringue pulls

HOW TO make a SOFT MeRINGue

Egg whites should be at room temperature. Beat egg whites on high speed in bowl of a heavy-duty mixer fitted with the whisk until soft peaks form.

Gradually add 2 tablespoons sugar for each egg white, 1 tablespoon at a time. Continue beating until glossy and stiff peaks form. When you lift the beaters, meringue should form peaks that remain upright. Rub a little meringue between your fingers to feel if the sugar is dissolved.

Soft meringue should be spread over a warm pie filling and sealed to the crust. Bake at 350°F until lightly browned.

moisture from the air that appear as tiny drops on its surface. It's also harder to dissolve the sugar in the egg whites.

LEAVENING

Leavening ingredients increase the volume and lightness of baked goods. Baking powder and baking soda are the most common leavening agents in baking. Double-acting baking powder acts twice—once when combined with a liquid and again when heated. Use it before the expiration date on the can. Baking soda reacts immediately with acids such as buttermilk, sour cream, and molasses in batters, so it's important to bake soon after adding the baking soda. Eggs can also be leavening agents.

SUGAR

Granulated sugar is the main sweetener in baking. It is produced from sugar cane and sugar beets. Sugar adds sweetness, tenderness, and moistness and aids in browning. Pure cane sugar has all the molasses boiled off during processing.

Brown sugar contains some molasses, which changes its flavor slightly. Light brown and dark brown sugar can be used interchangeably, although dark brown sugar has a more pronounced flavor. Store brown sugar tightly covered or it will dry out. Because of the molasses in brown sugar, recipes calling for it often contain baking soda. When measuring brown sugar, pack it into the measuring cup for the most accurate measure.

Powdered sugar, also called confectioner's sugar, has been ground finely and dissolves easily. It helps to sift powdered sugar when you are using it in frostings and glazes. Use powdered sugar only when specified in recipes, and never use it as a substitute for granulated sugar.

SALT

Salt provides flavor in baking and also controls the fermentation of yeast. It must be added during preparation because it can't be added after baking. Baked goods without salt taste flat. I use table salt because it dissolves easily. Kosher salt is coarser than table salt and weighs less, so when you substitute it for table salt, you must use more.

FATS

Butter is my preference for almost all my baking because it adds an unmistakable flavor to baked goods. I use salted butter for most recipes, and specify unsalted butter in recipes where the flavor difference is obvious such as in cakes and cookies. The amount of salt added is very small, so you can use salted and unsalted butter interchangeably without adjusting the salt quantity in your recipe. Soften butter by letting it stand at room temperature about 45 minutes. To soften it more quickly, cut the butter into small pieces and let them stand about 15 minutes. One pound of butter contains 2 cups, or 4 sticks. Each stick is equal to ½ cup. The paper wrapper on each stick is marked in tablespoons and is an easy way to measure.

Solid vegetable shortening (Crisco is one brand) is 100% fat and is often preferred in making pastry. Shortening doesn't have the delicate flavor of butter, and I don't use it often.

Margarine doesn't perform as well as butter, and all reduced-fat margarines and spreads are unsuitable for baking.

DAIRY INGREDIENTS

Milk and buttermilk are liquid ingredients used in many recipes. Use whole milk or 2% milk and lowfat buttermilk. Full-fat sour cream is used in all the recipes unless reduced-fat sour cream is specified. If you want to reduce the fat in something you are baking, you can experiment with low-fat products, but your results won't be the same.

Whipping cream or heavy whipping cream must contain 36% to 40% milk fat. I prefer the pasteurized over the ultra-pasteurized. Although the ultra-pasteurized has a longer shelf life, it doesn't whip as well. (See Side Bar)

> ## HOW TO WHIP CREAM
>
> For best results, chill both the mixer bowl and the whisk. Place whipping cream in the bowl of a heavy-duty mixer fitted with the whisk attachment.
>
> Whip whipping cream at High speed until soft peaks form. Scrape down sides of bowl. Add powdered sugar and vanilla, if desired. Continue beating until slightly stiff peaks form. Chill until served.

Always use high-quality cream cheese (such as Philadelphia brand), and don't use reduced-fat cream cheese or nonfat cream cheese for baking unless it's specified in the recipe.

YEAST

There are two basic kinds of yeast: active dry and compressed. I prefer active dry because it keeps a long time in the refrigerator and is easy to use. Always check the expiration date on yeast, and don't use it if it's past the date. Fast-rising yeast cuts rising time in half. It is convenient when you are short of time but many flavors develop during rising that are missing in breads made with fast-rising yeast.

Because yeast is alive and produces carbon dioxide as it grows, it is important to use the right temperature liquid so the yeast isn't killed. After adding the yeast to the warm water, you must wait about 5 minutes for the yeast to begin to grow. (This is called proofing because you are proving the yeast is alive.)

> ## HOW TO DISSOLVE yeast
>
> To dissolve yeast, sprinkle it over water that is between 105 and 115°F. (This should feel warm on the inside of your wrist.) Allow yeast to stand 5 minutes before adding it to the recipe.
>
> When yeast is to be added to part of the flour, it can be dissolved using warmer water (120 to 130°F). (This should feel slightly hot on the inside of your wrist.) Add the very warm water containing the yeast to the flour mixture .

Standard active dry yeast must be completely dissolved in warm water before using. (See Side Bar) To guarantee success, use an instant-read thermometer. A ¼-ounce envelope of yeast contains 2¼ teaspoons.

VANILLA

Almost every recipe contains vanilla. I even add a little vanilla to my chocolate recipes because I think it improves the overall flavor. Infusing vanilla beans into alcohol produces pure vanilla extract. Because the production of vanilla is labor-intensive, vanilla extract and beans are expensive. Fortunately vanilla is used here in small amounts and is worth the expense. The flavor of imitation vanilla extract is unlike the flavor of real vanilla, and I don't recommend using it. Choose vanilla beans that are soft and flexible, not dried out. After the seeds are removed from vanilla beans, I place the remaining bean in powdered sugar to make vanilla sugar.

CHOCOLATE

There are many brands of chocolate on the market and many choices. Choose a brand with a high amount of cocoa liquor or cocoa solids. Chocolate can develop "bloom," which appears as discoloration or streaks on the surface of the chocolate and is caused by change in storage temperatures. This chocolate can be melted and used with no change in quality of the end product.

Unsweetened chocolate, or bitter chocolate, produces the deepest chocolate flavor due to a high content of cocoa solids and cocoa butter.

Bittersweet and semisweet chocolate contain similar amounts of sugar, but bittersweet has more cocoa solids, which adds more chocolate flavor.

Semisweet chocolate chips are best used whole, not melted, because they are manufactured to keep their shape. When semisweet chocolate chips are called for in baked goods, most other kinds of chocolate chips can be substituted.

Milk chocolate contains sugar and milk solids and has a sweet, mellow flavor. It can't be used in melted form in baking, but when chopped, it is delicious in cookies.

White chocolate is usually labeled as a white baking bar. In the U.S., products without cocoa solids can't be labeled chocolate. Look for cocoa butter in the ingredients. White chips don't melt well but are perfect for cookies or bars.

HOW TO MELT CHOCOLATE

Place chopped chocolate in a medium bowl and set bowl over, not in, a saucepan with simmering water until chocolate melts. Or use a double boiler. The last little lumps will melt as the mixture sits. Cool slightly.

I also have melted chocolate in the microwave on Defrost power. You must be careful not to scorch it or it crumbles. When chocolate is melted in the microwave, its shape stays the same, so stir often.

Cocoa is also very high in cocoa solids and can be purchased unsweetened or sweetened (sweetened cocoa is used for hot beverages). Cocoa is naturally acidic and can be processed with alkali, making it milder. This is called Dutch-process cocoa.

Melting chocolate is best done in a bowl over hot water because it will melt slowly and be ready when you need it. Be careful not to get a drop of water in the chocolate or it will "seize" and form hard lumps. Chocolate can also be melted in the microwave. (See Side Bar)

HOW TO measure

Accurate measuring is essential for successful baking. Liquids should be measured in clear glass or plastic measuring cups that have spouts. With the cup placed on a flat surface, add the liquid and read the volume of the liquid at eye level.

Dry ingredients should be spooned into dry measuring cups (cups with exact measurements when filled to the top) and leveled off with a metal spatula or a straight edge. Before measuring flour, stir it with a spoon to lighten it. Spoon the flour into the measuring cup and scrape off the excess. If too much flour is packed into the cup, the baked product likely will be dry.

When measuring brown sugar, pack it into the measuring cup and then level it off. Pack it firmly enough so that it holds its shape when removed from the cup.

Spoon solid vegetable shortening into a dry measuring cup, pressing out any air pockets and leveling it off. Sour cream also is measured in dry measuring cups.

When using measuring spoons for dry ingredients, fill the spoon's bowl and then level it off. With liquid ingredients, just fill the bowl of the spoon.

TIPS FOR successful Baking

Read the entire recipe before beginning to bake.

Carefully follow the directions in the recipe.

Wait until you've made the recipe a few times before making changes. Don't make any substitutions in a recipe you are trying for the first time.

Use an oven thermometer, and adjust your oven as needed. If possible, adjust the thermostat on your oven. Or correct for any error by changing your oven setting.

Take a quick peek a few minutes before baking time is up and test for doneness.

chapter one

· ·

BISCUITS anD scones

YOU CAN'T BEAT OLD-FASHIONED baking powder biscuits: fragrant and steaming right from the oven, tender and flaky inside and golden brown on the outside. In America, scones are usually sweeter and flakier than biscuits and have become popular with the rise of coffee shops on every corner. Refrigerated biscuit dough, a modern convenience, is easy to use, but the results can't compare with homemade.

Biscuits are baked from ingredients almost everyone has in their pantry and refrigerator. Flour, baking powder, salt, and sometimes sugar, are pantry staples everywhere. Solid vegetable shortening and milk complete the essentials. Biscuits and scones are at their peak when they are freshly baked and dripping with butter and jam.

Biscuits, scones, and shortcakes depend on two key techniques for success: cutting in shortening or butter, and kneading with a light touch. The easiest method for cutting in shortening is with a pastry blender, but using a crisscross motion with two knives has similar results. A pastry blender has a round handle and 5 or 6 metal cutters with space between each, making it easy to cut up the fat and coat it with flour. For the flakiest biscuits or scones, leave some pieces about the size of peas.

After cutting in the fat with the pastry blender, press the flour mixture between your fingers and feel for any large lumps of fat. Rubbing these lumps of fat between your fingers with a little flour is a good way to test your expertise at cutting fat into flour. When the biscuits bake, the pea-sized pieces of fat melt and leave pockets that inflate, as they are filled with steam from the liquid in the dough.

Tender and light biscuits are baked from slightly moist, sticky dough that is handled gently and lightly kneaded. Add as little flour as possible during kneading, just enough to keep the dough from sticking to the surface and still form a soft dough. Gentle kneading forms the dough and develops enough gluten to give it the structure that allows the biscuits to rise during baking.

With the right amount of kneading, biscuits will rise when baked to almost double their height. The secret is not kneading the dough more than 10 times, even though you are tempted to do more. Pat out the dough to an even thickness, and press firmly with the biscuit cutter. For softer biscuits, place them close together in your baking pan; leave an inch between them on a baking sheet for crisper sides.

Biscuits and scones use double-acting baking powder as the leavening agent to make the biscuits rise. It's called double-acting because it acts twice, once when you add liquid and again during baking. Baking powder contains cream of tartar and baking soda that give off carbon dioxide when dissolved and heated. If you run out of baking powder, you can make your own:

Combine ½ teaspoon cream of tartar and ¼ teaspoon baking soda and use in place of 1 teaspoon baking powder.

Baking soda, which neutralizes the acid in the milk, aids in rising. Most bakers use vegetable shortening, such as Crisco, for biscuits because it makes them flakier. Butter or margarine also can be used, but biscuits will not be as tender because butter and margarine actually contain less fat than shortening.

Besides simple ingredients, biscuits and scones require little equipment. I highly recommend a pastry or dough blender, a biscuit cutter, and a heavy baking sheet. But you can also bake great biscuits using two knives to cut in the flour and an empty can as a biscuit cutter.

OLD-FASHIONED BAKING POWDER BISCUITS

Old-fashioned baking powder biscuits straight out of the oven are tender and flaky inside and golden brown on the outside. Dripping with lots of butter and spread with homemade strawberry jam there is nothing more comforting. What's the secret to tender biscuits? Only knead the dough 10 times, even though you are tempted to do more.

MAKES 8 BISCUITS

> 2 cups all-purpose flour
> 1 tablespoon baking powder
> ½ teaspoon salt
> ½ cup solid vegetable shortening
> ¾ cup milk

Heat the oven to 450°F with oven rack in middle.

Combine flour, baking powder, and salt in a medium bowl.

Cut in shortening with a pastry blender until mixture resembles coarse crumbs with some pea-sized pieces. Add milk and stir with a fork until clumps form, making slightly sticky dough.

Place dough on a well-floured work surface. Coat your hands with flour and knead gently 8 to 10 times, or toss dough a few times like a pizza, until the dough just holds together and is no longer sticky.

Gently pat dough into a 9-inch round at least ½ inch thick, lifting dough occasionally so it doesn't stick to the surface. Cut 2 ½ -inch biscuits with a biscuit cutter.

Place biscuits about 1 inch apart on an ungreased cookie sheet. Press any remaining scraps together and cut into biscuit-sized pieces.

Bake 10 to 12 minutes or until golden brown. Biscuits should have a golden brown crust, be light and tender with a slightly moist interior. Serve warm.

BAKER'S NOTES: You can use two table knives that are crossed and pulled through the shortening if you don't have a pastry blender.

Use an up and down motion to cut the biscuits—do not twist cutter back and forth. Dip the cutter into flour before each cut to make sharp cuts that ensure high-rising biscuits. An empty soup can is a great substitute for a biscuit cutter.

SECRETS TO SUCCESS: I never re-roll the scraps because too much handling makes the biscuits tough. I lightly press the scraps together and cut into biscuits.

Place the biscuits about 1 inch apart on the cookie sheet so the hot air can circulate during baking and form a crisp crust.

asiago BISCUIT TWISTS

These simple biscuits are loaded with flavor! I usually serve them when we are having a soup supper since they are easily made at the last minute, and they complement the flavor of many soups. These biscuits bake to a pretty golden brown.

MAKES 16 TWISTS

½ cup grated Asiago or Parmesan cheese
¼ cup butter or margarine, melted
2 cups all-purpose flour
1 tablespoon baking powder
½–1 teaspoon cracked peppercorns
½ teaspoon salt
⅓ cup solid vegetable shortening
¾ cup lowfat buttermilk

Heat oven to 450°F with oven rack in the middle. Place Asiago cheese and melted butter onto individual flat dishes and set aside.

Combine flour, baking powder, pepper, and salt in a medium bowl.

Cut in shortening with a pastry blender until mixture resembles coarse crumbs with some pea-sized pieces. Add buttermilk and stir with a fork until clumps form, making slightly sticky dough.

Place dough on a well-floured work surface. Coat your hands with flour and knead gently 8 to 10 times or toss dough a few times like a pizza until dough just holds together and is no longer sticky.

Gently pat dough into a 9-inch square about ½ inch thick. Lift dough occasionally and add a little flour underneath if it is sticking to the work surface.

Cut into 16 strips, each about ½ inch wide. Working with one strip at a time, dip strip into melted butter and then into Asiago cheese. Twist strip 3 or 4 times and place on cookie sheet.

Bake 10 to 14 minutes or until golden brown. Cool a couple of minutes on cookie sheet before removing to serve warm, or cool to room temperature.

BAKER'S NOTE: If you slightly press each end of the dough strips onto the cookie sheet, it helps keep the biscuit strips twisted.

SECRETS TO SUCCESS: Asiago cheese is an aged Italian cheese with a mild, nutty flavor similar to Parmesan cheese, which you can readily substitute.

cheesy DROP BISCUITS

I teach this recipe in one of my children's classes because it doesn't involve kneading—the soft dough is just dropped onto the cookie sheet. The dough spreads a little during baking, making the biscuits a little ragged, but they are still tender and flaky.

MAKES 12 BISCUITS

2 cups all-purpose flour
1 tablespoon baking powder
½ teaspoon salt
½ cup solid vegetable shortening
¾ cup milk
1 cup shredded sharp Cheddar cheese

Heat oven to 450°F with oven rack in middle. Spray a cookie sheet with nonstick cooking spray.

Combine flour, baking powder, and salt in a medium bowl.

Cut in shortening with a pastry blender until mixture resembles coarse crumbs with some pea-sized pieces. Add milk and stir with a fork until a slightly sticky dough forms. Stir in shredded cheese.

Drop dough from a spoon into 12 mounds about 2 inches apart on prepared cookie sheet.

Bake 10 to 12 minutes or until golden brown. Biscuits will have a ragged appearance and a golden brown crust, be light and tender, with a slightly moist interior. Serve warm.

BAKER'S NOTE: Sharp Cheddar cheese gives the best flavor but pepper jack and Parmesan cheese are nice variations.

Honey orange scones

American scones are usually slightly sweeter and richer than biscuits and shaped into a round loaf that is cut into wedges before baking. Scones are served warm for tea in Scotland and England with jam and clotted cream. Clotted cream has a rich and luxurious mouth feel because of the high percentage of butter fat—perfect with tender scones.

MAKES 8 SCONES

2 ¼ cups all-purpose flour
1 tablespoon baking powder
¾ teaspoon salt
½ cup solid vegetable shortening
½ cup milk
⅓ cup honey
1 tablespoon grated orange peel
½ cup powdered sugar
2–3 teaspoons orange juice

Heat oven to 400°F with oven rack in middle.

Combine flour, baking powder, and salt in a medium bowl.

Cut in shortening with a pastry blender until mixture resembles coarse crumbs with some pea-sized pieces.

Combine milk, honey, and orange peel in a small bowl. Add milk mixture to flour mixture, and stir with a fork until clumps form, making slightly sticky dough.

Place dough on a well- floured work surface. Coat your hands with flour and knead gently 8 to 10 times or toss dough a few times like a pizza until dough just holds together and is no longer sticky.

Gently pat dough into an 8-inch round about 1 inch thick, lifting dough occasionally so it doesn't stick to the surface.

Cut into 8 wedges. I always use a pizza cutter because it makes sharp cuts and keeps scones in the proper shape. Separate wedges slightly and place on an ungreased cookie sheet, keeping wedges about ½ inch apart in a circular pattern.

Bake 15 to 20 minutes or until golden brown. Remove from oven and cool on a wire cooling rack about 5 minutes. Remove from pan and place on cooling rack.

Combine powdered sugar and orange juice in a small bowl and stir until smooth. Add extra orange juice to make glaze thin enough for drizzling. Drizzle over warm scones. Serve warm or at room temperature.

BAKER'S NOTE: Spray the inside of a glass measuring cup with nonstick cooking spray before measuring the honey, and the honey will slide out easily.

SECRETS TO SUCCESS: One orange will yield about 1 tablespoon grated peel. Be sure to grate only the orange layer, not the white layer underneath.

Place a tray or waxed paper under the scones to catch the glaze.

BLUEBERRY CORNMEAL SCONES

Because of the blueberries in this dough, it is impossible to knead without breaking the berries and giving the dough an unappealing blue cast. I've eliminated that problem by dropping the dough directly onto the cookie sheet (which also makes the recipe super-fast). The cornmeal gives the scones a slightly crunchy texture. If you prefer a less sweet scone, reduce the brown sugar to ¼ cup.

MAKES 8 SCONES

1 ¾ cups all-purpose flour
½ cup cornmeal
⅓ cup brown sugar
1 tablespoon baking powder
½ teaspoon salt
⅓ cup butter, cut-up
⅔ cup milk
½ cup blueberries

Heat oven to 400°F with oven rack in middle. Grease a large cookie sheet and sprinkle with about 2 teaspoons cornmeal. (I like this because it adds a little more crunch to the scones, but the cornmeal can be omitted.)

Combine flour, cornmeal, brown sugar, baking powder, and salt in a medium bowl.

Cut in butter with a pastry blender until the mixture resembles coarse crumbs with some pea-sized pieces. Add milk and stir with a fork until a sticky dough forms.

Add blueberries and stir gently. Drop dough onto prepared sheet in 8 mounds, using about ⅓ cup for each.

Bake 16 to 20 minutes or until golden brown. Serve warm or at room temperature.

BAKER'S NOTE: If you substitute frozen blueberries for fresh, the berries should be used frozen and the baking time lengthened by a couple of minutes. I rinse frozen berries and pat them dry before adding them.

CHOCOLATE CHIP SCONES WITH STRAWBERRY BUTTER

Deep chocolate flavor and milk chocolate chips make these scones yummy. I created this recipe when two friends and I were giving an elegant tea as a bridal shower for a close friend. I cut small scones and served them warm with a scoop of the strawberry butter.

MAKES 12 SCONES

2 cups all-purpose flour

½ cup sugar

⅓ cup Dutch process cocoa

1 tablespoon baking powder

½ teaspoon salt

⅓ cup cold butter, cut into ½-inch pieces

1 cup whipping cream

1 teaspoon vanilla

1 cup milk chocolate chips

STRAWBERRY BUTTER

½ cup butter at room temperature

¼ cup powdered sugar

2 tablespoons strawberry jam

Heat oven to 400°F with oven rack in middle.

Combine flour, sugar, cocoa, baking powder, and salt in a medium bowl.

Cut in butter with a pastry blender until mixture resembles coarse crumbs with some pea-sized pieces.

Combine whipping cream and vanilla. Add to the flour mixture and stir with a fork until clumps form, making slightly sticky dough. Stir in chocolate chips.

Place dough on well-floured work surface. Knead gently 8 to 10 times or toss dough like a pizza until it holds together and is no longer sticky.

Roll or pat out dough to a thickness of about ½ inch. Cut scones with a 3-inch biscuit cutter. Press firmly with biscuit cutter to cut though the chocolate chips. If dough sticks, dip cutter in flour before each cut.

Place the scones on an ungreased cookie sheet. Sprinkle the tops with a little sugar.

Bake 14 to 18 minutes or until scones are no longer moist and are firm when pressed lightly with a finger. Serve at once or cool on wire cooling racks.

STRAWBERRY BUTTER

While the scones are baking, you can prepare the Strawberry Butter. Combine butter and powdered sugar in a small bowl and stir until smooth. Stir in jam and mix well.

BAKER'S NOTE: Make mini-scones by cutting the dough with a 2-inch biscuit cutter. I have a biscuit cutter with a scalloped edge that is especially festive. Because they are smaller they will bake in about 11 minutes.

SECRETS TO SUCCESS: The Dutch cocoa has been processed to neutralize the natural acidic flavor of cocoa and create a richer, deeper flavor in baked goods. Unsweetened cocoa is a good substitute.

"Sanding" sugar doesn't melt during baking and makes the tops of the scones sparkle. It can be purchased at specialty stores.

Peach Shortcake

Juicy ripe peaches say summer like nothing else. Although it can be hard to get ripe peaches, even when they are in season, I think it is well worth the effort—and the perfect showcase is tender flaky shortcake piled high with clouds of whipped cream. Shortcake is usually a little richer and more cake-like than biscuits because it contains more butter and a little sugar, but it is prepared using the same key techniques.

MAKES 6 SERVINGS

2 cups all-purpose flour
⅓ cup sugar
1 tablespoon baking powder
½ teaspoon salt
½ cup cold butter, cut into ½-inch pieces
½ cup milk
1 egg, beaten
4 cups sliced peeled fresh peaches
2 tablespoons sugar
1 teaspoon lemon juice
½ teaspoon almond extract
1 cup whipping cream
½ teaspoon vanilla
2 tablespoons powdered sugar

Heat oven to 425°F with oven rack in middle. Lightly grease a cookie sheet or spray with nonstick cooking spray.

Combine flour, ⅓ cup sugar, baking powder, and salt in a medium bowl.

Cut in butter with a pastry blender until mixture resembles coarse crumbs with some pea-sized pieces. Mix milk and egg. Add to flour mixture and stir with a fork until clumps form, making slightly sticky dough.

Place dough on a well-floured work surface. Coat your hands with flour and knead gently about 8 to 10 times or toss a few times like a pizza until dough just holds together and is no longer sticky.

Gently pat dough into a 9-inch round about ½ inch thick. Cut into 6 biscuits with 3-inch biscuit cutter.

Place shortcakes on prepared cookie sheet. Brush tops with milk and sprinkle with a little additional sugar.

Bake 12 to 15 minutes or until golden brown. Cool shortcakes about 2 minutes in pan before serving warm, or cool completely on wire cooling rack.

Combine peaches, 2 tablespoons sugar, lemon juice, and almond extract. Let stand about ½ hour until juicy. The lemon juice will prevent peaches from turning brown.

Whip the whipping cream on High speed in the bowl of a heavy-duty mixer fitted with whisk attachment until soft peaks form. Add vanilla and powdered sugar, and beat on Low speed until thickened.

Cut shortcakes in half horizontally. Place bottoms on serving plates. Cover with peaches and juice, add the tops, and mound high with whipped cream.

BAKER'S NOTES: Try chilling the bowl and beaters before beating the cold whipping cream. This helps the cream to whip faster and higher.

This dough is stickier than biscuit dough, so you may need to add more flour while kneading and cutting.

SECRETS TO SUCCESS: Store peaches at room temperature for a day or two after purchasing to allow ripening. I have the most success when I place them in a brown paper bag.

When I need just a little, I use lemon juice that is found in the freezer section of the supermarket. I like its flavor better than bottled lemon juice, and it keeps a long time in the refrigerator after thawing.

IRISH SODA BREAD

Traditional Irish soda bread usually contains currants or raisins, and which is authentic is a hot topic of debate among purists. I prefer golden raisins because their sweetness contrasts with the tangy buttermilk and adds an extra layer of flavor to the bread. Every year I bake this bread in March to celebrate St. Patrick's Day.

MAKES 2 LOAVES

3 cups all-purpose flour
1 cup whole wheat flour
½ cup sugar
1 tablespoon baking powder
1½ teaspoons baking soda
½ teaspoon salt
½ cup butter, cold, cut into ½-inch pieces
1½ cups lowfat buttermilk
1 cup golden raisins

Heat oven to 375°F with oven rack in middle. Lightly grease a large cookie sheet.

Combine flour, whole wheat flour, sugar, baking powder, baking soda, and salt in a large bowl.

Cut in butter with a pastry blender until mixture resembles coarse crumbs with some pea-sized pieces.

Add buttermilk and stir until clumps form, making a sticky dough with ragged edges. Stir in raisins.

Place dough on a well-floured work surface. Dust your hands with flour and knead gently 8 to 10 times or toss dough a few times like a pizza until it just holds together and is no longer sticky. Add a little flour as needed.

Gather dough together and cut roughly in half. Pat each half into a round loaf about 7 inches across. Place both loaves on the cookie sheet.

Bake 30 to 35 minutes or until deep golden brown with pebbly tops, no longer moist on the surface, but moist inside. Cool loaves on wire cooling racks. Allow loaves to cool at least 10 minutes before slicing.

BAKER'S NOTES: You can substitute two 9-inch round cake pans for the cookie sheet to help the loaves keep their round shape without changing baking time.

Because this is a sticky dough, you may need to add 1 to 2 tablespoons more flour than in other recipes.

SECRETS TO SUCCESS: You don't need to mix very much when adding the raisins, as the kneading will distribute them.

chapter two

MUFFINS, QUICK BREADS, AND POPOVERS

QUICK BREADS REFERS TO a group of easily prepared breakfast breads such as Banana Bran Bread and Everyday Blueberry Muffins that use baking powder for rising. Muffins, quick breads, and popovers are easy to make and can be on the table in less than an hour. They are usually served warm for breakfast or brunch with butter or another spread, such as honey, cream cheese, or jam. They also are great accompaniments to some main-dish salads.

This group of breads got the name "quick breads" when baking powder became available at the turn of the previous century. Prior to the use of baking powder, bread rose due to gas produced by yeast as it grew, a time-intensive process. Popovers and spoonbread are in this chapter because they also are quick to mix and surprisingly easy to bake. Leavened with steam from eggs and milk, they come out of the oven dramatically puffed and golden.

Muffins and quick breads are prepared using the same technique called the "muffin method." The dry ingredients and liquids are combined separately and then stirred together just until the dry ingredients are evenly moistened. The batter still might be lumpy, but lumps disappear during baking. When the batter is mixed too much, it increases the amount of gluten formed, creating tough muffins with peaked tops and tunnels inside.

Muffins and quick bread loaves are not as tender or as sweet as cakes because they contain much less fat and sugar. Although some recipes use butter because of its flavor, vegetable oil is probably more common. It produces muffins with a fine crumb and light texture. For the best results, some recipes contain both baking powder and baking soda, and it is important to follow those recipes carefully. Muffins and quick breads can keep for several days at room temperature if they are well wrapped; they also freeze easily and remain moist.

With some planning the evening before, muffins hot from the oven can be served first thing in the morning. Measure the dry ingredients the night before, and combine the liquids in the morning as the oven heats. I don't use paper liners for muffins because the muffins tend to stick to the paper, and I like the slightly crisp crust that develops without the paper liners.

Spray the cups of a standard muffin pan with nonstick cooking spray, spraying a little on the space between the cups, to make it easy to remove the muffins. A small ice cream scoop (No. 16, ¼ cup) fills the muffin cups quickly and uniformly. My recipes are designed to make a dozen muffins, but if you divide the batter into 10 muffins and bake a couple of minutes longer, you can make larger muffins. Perfect muffins have a rounded pebbly top and a tender golden-brown crust. The interior should be slightly moist and have a uniform texture.

The batter for quick breads is similar to muffin batter and is prepared the same way, but it is baked in a loaf pan. Both batters often include fruit and nuts. Many quick breads will have a crack down the center that occurs during baking, but this doesn't affect the quality of the bread. Quick breads are usually easier to slice the second day. Because of their tenderness, slice them with a serrated knife or an electric knife.

Muffins are baked in standard muffin pans (also called cupcake pans) or mini- or jumbo-muffin pans. A standard muffin pan has twelve 2½ x 1¼-inch cups. Most recipes make 12 muffins, 24 mini-muffins, or 6 jumbo muffins, and it's nice to have a variety of pans.

Quick breads are usually baked in 9 x 5-inch loaf pans, but I often use mini-loaf pans (5¾ x 3¼ inches) because I can freeze one or two mini-loaves and use them later. Having a variety of loaf pans makes it easy to adjust the sizes and number of the loaves in a recipe. Popover pans make the best popovers, but custard cups or a muffin pan also can be used.

cinnamon streusel muffins

One of the reasons muffins are so popular is because they are quick and easy to make and full of flavor. Adding the liquid all at once to the dry ingredients actually is called the "muffin method" and makes muffins that are light and tender with an even texture inside. Serve these muffins warm from the oven with apple butter to enhance their spicy cinnamon flavor.

MAKES 12 MUFFINS

STREUSEL TOPPING

¼ cup all-purpose flour
¼ cup firmly packed brown sugar
1 teaspoon cinnamon
3 tablespoons cold butter

MUFFINS

2 cups all-purpose flour
½ cup sugar
¼ cup firmly packed brown sugar
1 tablespoon baking powder
1 teaspoon cinnamon
½ teaspoon salt
¾ cup milk
½ cup butter, melted
1 teaspoon vanilla
1 egg, beaten

Heat oven to 400°F with oven rack in middle. Lightly spray 12 cups in a standard muffin pan with nonstick cooking spray.

STREUSEL TOPPING

Combine flour, brown sugar, and cinnamon in a small bowl. Cut in butter with a pastry blender until mixture resembles coarse crumbs with some pea-sized pieces.

MUFFINS

Combine flour, sugar, brown sugar, baking powder, cinnamon, and salt in a large bowl. Make a well in center of the flour by pushing ingredients out toward sides of bowl.

Combine milk, melted butter, vanilla, and egg in a medium bowl. Pour milk mixture into the flour mixture, and stir only until the flour is moistened even though the batter is not smooth. Scrape down sides of bowl.

Divide batter into prepared muffin cups, filling them about ⅔ full. Sprinkle about 1 tablespoon of streusel over each muffin.

Bake 18 to 20 minutes or until golden brown and a toothpick inserted in the center of a couple of muffins comes out dry. Cool slightly and remove from the pan.

Run a small metal spatula around edge of each muffin to loosen it, and lift gently from the pan. Serve muffins warm with butter or jam.

BAKER'S NOTE: For muffins, I prefer spraying the muffin cups instead of using paper liners because the muffins usually stick to the paper.

SECRETS TO SUCCESS: Muffins are at their best served warm from the oven. Any uneaten muffins can be wrapped and stored at room temperature. I reheat them in the microwave before serving.

---

everyday blueberry muffins

What's your favorite fruit muffin? After you prepare this basic blueberry muffin recipe, try substituting chopped apples or chopped strawberries for the blueberries. The muffin remains the same—only the fruit changes. For blueberry muffins, I use butter as the fat for the flavor.

MAKES 12 MUFFINS

> 2 cups all-purpose flour
> ½ cup sugar
> 1 tablespoon baking powder
> 1 teaspoon cinnamon
> ½ teaspoon salt
> ¾ cup milk
> ⅓ cup butter, melted
> 1 teaspoon vanilla
> 1 egg, beaten
> 1 cup fresh blueberries

Heat oven to 400°F with oven rack in middle. Spray 12 cups of a standard muffin pan with nonstick cooking spray.

Mix flour, sugar, baking powder, cinnamon, and salt in a large bowl. Make a well in center of the flour by pushing ingredients out toward sides of bowl.

Combine milk, melted butter, vanilla, and egg in a medium bowl with a wire whisk. Pour milk mixture into flour mixture, and stir only until flour is moistened even though the batter is not smooth. Scrape down sides of bowl.

Fold in blueberries, being careful not to break them or the batter will become blue.

Divide batter into sprayed muffin cups, using a scant ¼ cup of batter in each cup. Cups are usually filled about ¾ full.

Bake 15 to 20 minutes or until golden brown and a toothpick inserted in center of a couple of muffins comes out dry. Cool slightly and remove from pan.

Run a small metal spatula around edge of each muffin to loosen them and lift gently from the pan. Serve muffins warm with butter or jam and wait for the compliments!

BAKER'S NOTE: The muffin cups should all have about the same amount of batter so that they bake evenly. You can transfer batter to different cups to even them out, but minimize such activity or the muffins will be tough.

SECRETS TO SUCCESS: Muffins should be lightly rounded with a pebbly top and moist and tender inside.

If the muffins are left in the muffin cups too long, they will become soggy on the bottom.

HONEY-GLAZED APPLESAUCE MUFFINS

The buttery honey glaze on these muffins is what sets them apart. Before brushing the muffins with the glaze, allow them to cool slightly, and treat them gently or they will crumble because they are so tender. These muffins stay moist several days because the honey and applesauce prevent them from drying out.

MAKES 12 MUFFINS

MUFFINS

> 1 ½ cups all-purpose flour
> 3 teaspoons baking powder
> 2 teaspoons pumpkin pie spice
> ½ teaspoon salt
> 1 cup applesauce
> ⅓ cup vegetable oil
> ½ cup honey
> 1 egg, beaten

HONEY GLAZE

> ¼ cup butter, melted
> ¼ cup honey

Heat oven to 400°F with oven rack in middle. Spray a 12-cup standard muffin baking pan with nonstick cooking spray.

MUFFINS

Combine flour, baking powder, pumpkin pie spice, and salt in a large bowl. Make a well in center of the flour by pushing ingredients out toward sides of bowl.

Combine applesauce, oil, honey, and egg in a medium bowl with a wire whisk. Pour applesauce mixture into flour mixture, and stir only until flour is moistened even though batter is not smooth. Scrape down sides of bowl.

Fill muffin cups, using about ¼ cup of batter. Bake 18 to 23 minutes or until lightly browned and a toothpick inserted in a muffin comes out dry.

Cool muffins about 2 minutes. Run a metal spatula around each muffin to loosen it, lift gently from the bottom and remove from pan. Place muffins on wire cooling rack. I always put a piece of waxed paper under the rack to catch any honey glaze that drips.

Honey Glaze

For the glaze, whisk melted butter and ¼ cup honey in a small bowl until a glaze forms. Brush glaze generously over tops of warm muffins. Serve muffins warm or cool to room temperature.

BAKER'S NOTE: Pumpkin pie spice contains cinnamon, ginger, nutmeg, and cloves. Ordinary cinnamon may be used as a substitute.

SECRETS TO SUCCESS: I measure the oil first in a glass measuring cup and then measure the honey in the same cup. The honey slides right out of the oiled cup.

RaISIn BRan MUFFInS

One of these jumbo muffins is almost a complete breakfast. Sunflower nuts contain protein and iron in addition to adding a nice crunch. I like to serve them right out of the oven with a little honey butter.

MAKES 6 JUMBO MUFFINS

1 cup all-purpose flour
1 cup whole wheat flour
¼ cup firmly packed brown sugar
2 teaspoons baking powder
1 teaspoon cinnamon
½ teaspoon baking soda
¼ teaspoon salt
1 cup lowfat buttermilk
⅓ cup vegetable oil
½ cup honey
1 egg, beaten
2 cups raisin bran cereal, lightly crushed
⅓ cup sunflower nuts

Heat oven to 375°F with oven rack in center. Lightly spray 6 cups in a jumbo muffin pan with nonstick cooking spray.

Mix all-purpose flour, whole wheat flour, brown sugar, baking powder, cinnamon, baking soda, and salt in a large bowl. Make a well in center of the flour by pushing ingredients out toward sides of bowl.

Combine buttermilk, oil, honey and egg in a medium bowl. Pour buttermilk mixture into flour mixture, and stir only until the flour is moistened even though batter is not smooth. Scrape down sides of bowl.

Stir in raisin bran cereal and sunflower nuts, and mix just until blended.

Divide batter into prepared muffin cups, filling about ¾ full.

Bake 20 to 23 minutes or until golden brown and a toothpick inserted in center of a couple of muffins comes out dry. Cool in pan about 5 minutes.

Run a small metal spatula around edge of each muffin to loosen them, and gently lift muffins from pan. Cool on wire cooling rack. Serve warm.

BAKER'S NOTE: Because these muffins don't rise much, you can fill the cups fairly full. If you don't have a jumbo muffin pan, divide the batter into 12 muffin cups. Bake at 400°F about 18 to 20 minutes.

SECRETS TO SUCCESS: Don't buy the sunflower seeds or you'll have to shell them. Sunflower nuts can be plain or salted. I use the salted nuts but unsalted work just as well.

After measuring the cereal, crush it lightly with a rolling pin before adding it to the batter.

CORNMEAL MUFFINS

These muffins don't rise as high as other muffins and have a coarser texture because of the cornmeal. I always make these muffins when I'm serving chili for dinner because they are not very sweet, and the corn flavor complements the spicy chili. If you like sweeter muffins, increase the sugar to ⅓ cup.

MAKES 12 MUFFINS

1 cup all-purpose flour
1 cup cornmeal
¼ cup sugar
2 teaspoons baking powder
½ teaspoon baking soda
¼ teaspoon salt
1 cup lowfat buttermilk
¼ cup vegetable oil
1 egg, beaten

Heat oven to 400°F with oven rack in middle. Lightly spray the 12 cups of a standard muffin pan with nonstick cooking spray.

Combine flour, cornmeal, sugar, baking powder, baking soda, and salt in a large bowl. Make a well in center of the flour by pushing ingredients out toward sides of bowl.

Combine buttermilk, oil, and egg in a medium bowl. Pour buttermilk mixture into flour mixture, and stir only until the flour is evenly moistened even though batter is not smooth.

Divide batter into prepared muffin cups, using a scant ¼ cup batter in each cup.

Bake 12 to 16 minutes or until golden brown and a toothpick inserted in center of a couple of muffins comes out dry. Cool 3 minutes.

Run a small metal spatula around edge of each muffin to loosen them, and lift gently from pan. Cool on wire cooling rack. Serve muffins warm with butter and chili.

> BAKER'S NOTE: You can experiment with yellow, white, or blue cornmeal. Although they each have a distinctive color, their flavor is very similar. Yellow cornmeal contains more Vitamin A than white or blue. Blue cornmeal is usually found in specialty stores.
>
> SECRETS TO SUCCESS: If muffins are left in the pan too long, the bottoms will become soggy.

RHUBARB BREAD

. . . .

Although fresh rhubarb is available only in the spring, frozen rhubarb is available year round. Look for fresh rhubarb at farmers' markets and super-markets early in the spring. In this quick bread the tart flavor of the fruit contrasts with the spiciness of the nutmeg.

MAKES 1 LOAF (12 to 16 slices)

    2½ cups all-purpose flour
     ¼ cup sugar
      1 teaspoon baking soda
     ½ teaspoon salt
     ½ teaspoon grated fresh nutmeg, if desired
     ¾ cup firmly packed brown sugar
      1 cup lowfat buttermilk
     ½ cup vegetable oil
      2 eggs, beaten
    1½ cups fresh or frozen chopped rhubarb

Heat oven to 350°F with oven rack in middle. Lightly spray bottom of a 9 x 5-inch loaf pan with nonstick cooking spray.

Combine flour, sugar, baking soda, salt, and nutmeg in a large bowl. Make a well in center of the flour by pushing ingredients out toward sides of bowl.

Combine brown sugar, buttermilk, oil, and eggs in medium bowl, breaking up any small lumps in the brown sugar. Pour buttermilk mixture into the flour mixture, and stir only until the flour is evenly moistened even though batter is not smooth.

Stir rhubarb into the batter, pour into prepared pan, and smooth top. The pan will be about ¾ full, but it won't overflow.

Bake 55 to 70 minutes or until golden brown and a toothpick inserted in center comes out dry. The bread may begin to pull away from pan sides.

Cool on wire cooling rack 10 minutes. Run a spatula around sides of pan to loosen bread. Place rack over the bread and invert so bread falls onto the rack. Remove pan and turn top side up. The bread must cool before it can be sliced.

BAKER'S NOTES: Like any quick bread, this bread is easier to slice the second day. After cooling completely, wrap in plastic wrap and store at room temperature overnight.

As a substitute for buttermilk, you can place 2 teaspoons lemon juice or distilled vinegar in a glass measuring cup and add milk to make 1 cup. Let the mixture stand a couple of minutes.

SECRET TO SUCCESS: Frozen rhubarb doesn't need to be thawed before baking but does need to be chopped because the pieces are very large. Use a sharp knife, and chop it while it is still frozen. Do not use a food processor because it makes the rhubarb stringy.

banana bran bread

Bananas, bran cereal, and apricots all contribute healthy fiber to this updated classic. Use very ripe bananas—the skins can be totally brown—for the best banana flavor and the most sweetness. Quick breads have a denser texture than muffins, but it still is important not to stir too much.

MAKES 1 LOAF (12 to 16 slices)

> 1 ½ cups all-purpose flour
> ½ cup sugar
> 2 teaspoons baking powder
> ½ teaspoon baking soda
> ½ teaspoon salt
> 1 cup mashed, peeled bananas (about 2 large)
> ½ cup butter, melted
> ½ cup sour cream
> ¼ cup milk
> 2 eggs, beaten
> ½ cup high-fiber cereal with natural wheat bran (All Bran is one brand)
> ½ cup chopped dried apricots

Heat oven to 350°F with oven rack in middle. Lightly spray bottom of a 9 x 5-inch loaf pan with nonstick cooking spray.

Mix flour, sugar, baking powder, baking soda, and salt in a large bowl. Make a well in center of the flour by pushing ingredients out toward sides of bowl.

Combine bananas, butter, sour cream, milk, and eggs in a medium bowl with a wire whisk.

Pour banana mixture into flour mixture, and stir only until flour is evenly moistened even though batter is not smooth. Stir in cereal and apricots.

Pour batter into prepared pan and smooth the top. Bake 50 to 60 minutes or until golden brown and a toothpick inserted in center comes out dry. The bread may begin to pull away from pan sides.

Cool on wire cooling rack 10 minutes. Run a spatula around sides of pan to loosen bread. Place rack over the bread and invert so bread falls onto the rack. Remove pan and turn top side up. Cool before slicing.

> BAKER'S NOTE: The bananas can be mashed with a fork or an electric mixer. If the bananas are very ripe, I usually just mash with a fork; they don't have to be completely smooth.
>
> SECRET TO SUCCESS: I prefer California dried apricots to Mediterranean apricots, but either will do. Use scissors to cut the apricots.

CHOCOLATE ZUCCHINI BREAD

Zucchini is so easy to grow that every gardener has lots more than they can use. Baking zucchini bread is a great way to use extra quantities, and adding chocolate improves the flavor for non-zucchini enthusiasts. I shred the squash in my food processor, but it can be grated by hand.

MAKES 2 LOAVES (12 to 16 slices)

> 2 cups all-purpose flour
> 2 teaspoons cinnamon
> 1 teaspoon baking powder
> 1 teaspoon baking soda
> ½ teaspoon salt

1 ½ cups sugar

¾ cup vegetable oil

2 ounces unsweetened chocolate, melted and cooled

½ teaspoon vanilla

3 eggs, beaten

2 cups grated zucchini (2 medium zucchini)

¾ cup semisweet chocolate chips

Heat oven to 350°F with oven rack in middle. Grease with shortening and flour the bottom and part-way up sides of two 9 x 5-inch loaf pans.

Combine flour, cinnamon, baking powder, baking soda, and salt in a large bowl. Make a well in center of the flour by pushing ingredients out toward sides of bowl.

Combine sugar, oil, chocolate, vanilla, and eggs in a large bowl and whisk until smooth.

Pour chocolate mixture into flour mixture, and stir only until flour is evenly moistened even though batter is not smooth. Stir in zucchini and chocolate chips. Divide batter between the two prepared pans, and smooth the tops.

Bake 36 to 42 minutes or until a toothpick inserted in center comes out dry. The edges of the bread may be pulling away from pan sides.

Cool on wire cooling rack 10 minutes. Run a spatula around sides of pans to loosen bread. Place rack over the bread and invert so bread falls onto the rack. Remove pan and turn top side up. The bread must cool before it can be sliced, and it slices better the second day.

BAKER'S NOTE: When grating the zucchini by hand, absorb extra moisture by placing the shredded squash between paper towels.

SECRET TO SUCCESS: If the level of the batter isn't the same in both pans, one of the pans will bake quicker than the other. Take a quick peek after 30 minutes to check the doneness.

aLMOND Tea LOaF

A sweet glaze echoes the almond flavor of this sweet tea bread. Almond paste, which can be found in the baking section of most supermarkets, adds sweetness and texture to this tea bread and makes it unique. Look for it with the fruit fillings in the baking section.

MAKES 1 LOAF (12 to 16 slices)

1½ cups all-purpose flour
¾ cup sugar
2 teaspoons poppy seed
1 teaspoon baking powder
¼ teaspoon salt
½ cup butter, room temperature
¾ cup milk
2 eggs
1 teaspoon almond extract
½ teaspoon vanilla
½ cup crumbled almond paste, from a 7-ounce package

GLaze

½ cup sugar
¼ cup orange juice
1 teaspoon almond extract
½ teaspoon vanilla

Heat oven to 350°F with oven rack in middle. Lightly spray a 9 x 5-inch loaf pan with nonstick cooking spray.

Place flour, sugar, poppy seed, baking powder, salt, butter, milk, eggs, almond extract, and vanilla in bowl of a heavy-duty mixer. Beat on Low speed until blended.

Increase to Medium speed and beat 2 minutes, scraping sides of bowl occasionally. The batter will be smooth. Add almond paste. (If it is very firm, I usually chop it finely in my food processor.) Pour batter into prepared pan.

Bake 50 to 60 minutes or until golden brown and a toothpick inserted in center comes out dry. The bread may be beginning to pull away from pan sides.

Cool on wire cooling rack 10 minutes. Run a spatula around sides of pan to loosen bread. Place rack over the bread and invert so bread falls onto the rack. Remove pan and turn top side up. Place a tray or waxed paper beneath to catch the glaze.

GLAZE

Combine glaze ingredients in a small saucepan and heat until sugar is dissolved. Simmer 30 seconds. Pierce bread generously with a skewer. Slowly spoon warm glaze on top of bread, allowing it to soak in. Cool completely before slicing.

BAKER'S NOTE: Almond paste is made from ground almonds, sugar, and glycerin. It needs to be broken up, and I usually do this in my mini-food processor. It can also be grated with a hand grater. After opening, re-wrap it tightly and store it in your freezer.

SECRETS TO SUCCESS: Because this bread requires all ingredients to be beaten at once, it is essential to have the butter at room temperature.

I use a bamboo skewer to pierce the bread, but you can also use a two-pronged fork. The more you pierce the bread, the more glaze it can absorb.

HARVEST BALL PUMPKIN BREAD

I got this recipe from a friend with whom I worked when I was first out of college. It has been a family favorite ever since, and we look forward to it every autumn. The orange flavor is a surprising addition that works well with the spices.

MAKES 2 LOAVES (12 to 16 slices each)

2 cups all-purpose flour
1½ cups sugar
1 teaspoon baking powder
½ teaspoon baking soda
1 teaspoon cinnamon
¼ teaspoon salt
¼ teaspoon ground allspice
¼ teaspoon ground ginger
1 cup canned pumpkin
½ cup vegetable oil
⅓ cup orange juice
1 teaspoon grated orange peel
2 eggs, beaten
½ cup chopped pecans, optional

Heat oven to 350°F with oven rack in middle. Grease and flour the bottom and part-way up sides of two 9 x 5-inch loaf pans.

Combine flour, sugar, baking powder, baking soda, cinnamon, salt, allspice, and ginger in a large bowl. Make a well in center of the flour by pushing ingredients out toward sides of bowl.

Combine pumpkin, oil, orange juice, and orange peel in a large bowl. Pour pumpkin mixture into flour mixture, and stir only until flour is moistened even though batter is not smooth. Scrape down sides of bowl.

Add eggs, one at a time, and beat batter with a wire whisk after each addition until smooth. Stir in pecans.

Divide batter into prepared pans and smooth tops.

Bake 36 to 40 minutes or until a toothpick inserted in center comes out dry. The bread may be beginning to pull away from pan sides.

Cool on wire cooling rack 10 minutes. Run a spatula around sides of pans to loosen loaves. Place rack over the bread and invert so bread falls onto the rack. Remove pan and turn top side up. Cool completely before slicing.

BAKER'S NOTE: You can use 1½ teaspoons pumpkin pie spice instead of the spices listed.

SECRETS TO SUCCESS: Always grate the orange peel before cutting the orange and squeezing the juice.

easy cheesy popovers

Popovers are the drama queens of baking, always making a great impression when they enter the room. They are actually easy to make. Once you've baked popovers and see how easy it is, you'll probably want to get a popover pan, even though it's not required. With Swiss cheese and mustard, popovers are a great accompaniment to soups or main-dish salads.

MAKES 6 POPOVERS

> 1 cup all-purpose flour
> ½ teaspoon salt
> ½ teaspoon dry mustard
> 2 eggs, room temperature
> 1¼ cups warm milk
> 1 tablespoon butter, melted
> ½ cup grated Swiss cheese

Place flour, salt, and dry mustard in blender container. Pulse once or twice. Add eggs, warm milk, and butter. Blend on High about 10 seconds until smooth. Scrape down sides of container and blend again.

Stir in Swiss cheese. Cover batter and let it stand at room temperature about 20 minutes.

Heat oven to 450°F with oven rack in middle. Generously spray 6 cups in popover pan or a nonstick jumbo muffin pan with nonstick cooking spray.

Pour batter evenly into cups. Place pan in oven, and reduce oven temperature to 400°F. Don't open oven during baking.

Bake 25 to 35 minutes or until popovers are puffed, a deep golden brown, and no longer moist on the surface. Cool slightly on wire cooling rack before removing from pans. Serve popovers immediately with butter.

> BAKER'S NOTE: After you've made popovers a few times, you will know how you prefer them—moist and eggy inside or dry and crispy. Moist popovers collapse more quickly. For drier popovers, pierce them with the tip of a knife to allow steam to escape, and place them back in the turned-off oven for a few minutes.
>
> SECRETS TO SUCCESS: You can prepare the popover batter without using a blender. Combine all the ingredients in a medium bowl and mix with a wire whisk until smooth.

POPOVERS WITH BERRIES AND WHIPPED CREAM

Because these popovers are a little sweet, they are delicious for breakfast or brunch. If you don't have a popover pan, a muffin pan is an easy substitute. If you use a muffin pan, place batter in the four corner and two middle cups.

MAKES 6 POPOVERS

1 cup all-purpose flour
1 tablespoon sugar
¼ teaspoon salt
2 eggs, room temperature
1¼ cups warm milk
1 teaspoon vanilla
1 tablespoon butter, melted
1 quart strawberries, cleaned and sliced
1 cup whipping cream, whipped (see page 10)

Heat oven to 450°F with oven rack in middle. Generously spray 6 cups in a popover pan or a nonstick jumbo muffin pan with nonstick cooking spray.

Place flour, sugar, and salt in blender container. Pulse once or twice. Add eggs, warm milk, vanilla, and butter. Blend on High about 10 seconds until smooth. Scrape down sides of container and blend again. Cover batter and let stand at room temperature about 20 minutes.

Pour batter evenly into cups. I use a ladle of batter for each cup. Place pan in oven, and reduce oven temperature to 400°F. Don't open oven during baking.

Bake 25 to 35 minutes or until popovers are puffed, deep golden brown, and no longer moist on the surface.

Cool slightly on wire cooling rack before removing from pans. Serve immediately with fresh berries and whipped cream.

BAKER'S NOTES: I've had the best results when I've used nonstick cooking spray to coat the cups.

For breakfast, I serve hot popovers with maple syrup or cherry filling and sour cream.

German apple pancake

Whether you call this a "German" pancake or a "Dutch Baby," it's one of my favorite breakfast treats. It is puffed and golden brown when it comes out of the oven, but it deflates quickly. At a local restaurant that is famous for these pancakes, the server rushes to the table delivering the pancake while it is puffed and hot. When my children were younger, we'd often have this for dinner because it was one thing everybody loved! Powdered sugar is enough of a finishing touch, but we have been known to top it with maple syrup.

MAKES 4 SERVINGS

>   1 cup milk
> ½ cup all-purpose flour
>   2 tablespoons sugar
>   4 eggs, room temperature
>   2 tablespoons butter, melted
>   1 teaspoon vanilla
> ⅓ cup butter
> ½ cup sugar
>   1 cup sliced, peeled apple (1 medium)
>   1 teaspoon cinnamon
>   Powdered sugar

Place milk, flour, sugar, and eggs in blender container and blend until smooth. Scrape down sides of container, and add 2 tablespoons melted butter and vanilla and blend briefly. Let batter sit at room temperature 20 to 30 minutes, or refrigerate until needed.

Heat oven to 450°F with oven rack in middle. Place the ⅓ cup butter and ½ cup sugar in a 9-inch skillet and cook over low heat until butter is melted.

Add apples and sprinkle with cinnamon. Cook over low heat about 3 minutes or until apples begin to soften. Add batter and continue to cook until edges begin to set.

Place skillet in oven. Reduce oven temperature to 400°F. Don't open oven door during baking.

Bake 20 to 24 minutes or until pancake is puffed, deep golden brown, and no longer moist on the surface. Sprinkle with powdered sugar before serving. Serve immediately, as pancake deflates quickly.

BAKER'S NOTE: The batter can be refrigerated overnight. Remove it from the refrigerator before preparing the apple.

SECRETS TO SUCCESS: Use an apple that is recommended for cooking, such as a Golden Delicious. It is important to cook the apple slightly before adding the batter so that is cooked through.

If you don't have a blender, just combine the milk, flour, sugar, and eggs for the batter in a large bowl and whisk until smooth. Then add the melted butter and vanilla.

SOUTHERN-STYLE SPOONBREAD

I first tasted spoonbread in one of the taverns at Colonial Williamsburg many years ago. We were living in Washington, D.C., at the time and a friend at work shared her recipe with me. For a dinner featuring Southern favorites, I serve smoked ham, mashed sweet potatoes, and spoonbread.

MAKES 4 TO 6 SERVINGS

> 3 cups milk
> 1 cup cornmeal
> 1 teaspoon coarse salt
> 3 tablespoons butter
> 2 eggs, separated

Heat oven to 400°F with oven rack in middle. Lightly spray a 1½-quart casserole.

Combine milk, cornmeal, and salt in a medium saucepan. Heat over medium-high heat, whisking constantly, until mixture comes to a boil. Reduce heat to low, and boil 5 minutes, stirring often, until very thick. Stir across bottom and into corners of pan. Use a long handled spoon to avoid being spattered.

Remove cornmeal from heat, add butter, and let stand 5 minutes, stirring occasionally.

Beat egg yolks in a medium bowl. Remove about 1 cup of cornmeal from saucepan and slowly beat it into the eggs. After yolks are warmed, add egg mixture back into cornmeal mixture and beat until smooth.

Place egg whites in the bowl of a heavy-duty mixer and mix on High until soft peaks form when beaters are lifted. Fold egg whites into the cornmeal mixture, and spoon batter into the casserole .

Bake 40 to 50 minutes or until puffed and lightly browned and a knife inserted near center comes out clean, although it will be wet. Serve at once because spoonbread deflates quickly, but be careful you don't burn your mouth because it is very hot.

> BAKER'S NOTE: Use an oven mitt and a long-handled spoon to avoid being burned as you stir the cornmeal because it splatters.
>
> SECRETS TO SUCCESS: The only difficult part of this dish is adding the egg yolks to the hot cornmeal. It is important to add it slowly, with lots of stirring, so that the egg yolks don't cook and curdle.

chapter three

coffee cakes

COFFEE CAKES, TENDER SWEET CAKES covered with crumbly streusel topping and served warm for breakfast, are an American tradition. Other cultures serve similar sweets, but they are more likely to be presented in the afternoon with tea, coffee, and conversation. Both work well as a hospitable way to visit with family and friends. Coffee cakes are the sweetest of the quick breads, rising high from the use of baking powder and/or baking soda and rich in buttery flavor.

The quality of a homemade coffee cake just out of the oven makes a cake out of a bakery box seem a poor substitute. What could be a better way to start the day than biting into fresh fruit surrounded by a warm, tender cake? Brown sugar provides some caramel flavor, pecans or almonds add some crunch, and cinnamon adds a spicy accent.

As with all home baked goods, use only the highest quality ingredients. Although some of my recipes use shortening, I mostly rely on real butter for its unique flavor. Sour cream and buttermilk also add richness and tang. You can experiment with reduced-fat sour cream, but I don't recommend using fat-free as it adversely affects the texture of the bread.

There is an easy substitute for buttermilk: add 1 teaspoon lemon juice or white vinegar to a glass measuring cup and top with milk. In addition, you can purchase dried buttermilk that should be added with the dry ingredients. Water then replaces the liquid. I always keep a can readily available in my freezer because freezing adds to its storage life.

These homespun breakfast breads are assembled using square baking pans, loaf pans, Bundt pans, and springform pans. When you purchase a Bundt pan, buy a 10-cup, non-stick model. The non-stick coating helps release all the curves that make a Bundt cake so pretty. Because of the tenderness of coffee cakes, it is usually impossible to turn them out of the pan in one piece, which is why I sometimes use springform pans. The sides are easy to release, the bottom of the pan supports the cake, and you can cut pretty slices. In addition, a pastry blender is helpful, and a serrated knife makes it easier to slice the cake.

The techniques learned and practiced in this chapter include cutting in the butter, which is the same as the technique used for biscuits, streusel toppings, and pie crust. While the butter and sugar are creamed the same way as in cakes, the process is shorter because the texture sought is not as fine. The more you bake, the easier it will be to determine doneness, but color is a good guideline here.

GRANDMA'S OLD-FASHIONED COFFEE CAKE

Coffee cakes are richer than muffins and quick breads but not as tender or as sweet as cakes. Easy to make and always welcome, a coffee cake with this kind of topping is often called a crumb cake. It is a great recipe for beginning bakers because the preparation is simple. The spicy cinnamon aroma and flavor remind me of Sunday mornings when I was a child and we had a large breakfast after church.

MAKES 9 TO 12 SERVINGS

TOPPING

½ cup sugar
⅓ cup all-purpose flour
1 teaspoon cinnamon
¼ cup cold butter, cut-up

CAKE

1 ½ cups all-purpose flour
¾ cup sugar
1 teaspoon cinnamon
1 teaspoon baking powder
¼ teaspoon salt
¼ cup cold butter, cut-up
½ cup milk
1 egg, beaten
1 teaspoon vanilla

Heat oven to 375°F with oven rack in middle. Lightly spray bottom of a 9 x 9-inch baking pan with nonstick cooking spray.

TOPPING

Combine sugar, flour, and cinnamon in bowl of a heavy-duty mixer. Add butter and beat on Medium speed until mixture resembles coarse crumbs with some pea-sized pieces. Place crumb topping in a small bowl.

CAKE

In the same bowl, mix flour, sugar, cinnamon, baking powder, and salt. Add butter and beat on Medium speed until mixture resembles coarse crumbs with some pea-sized pieces.

Combine milk, egg, and vanilla in a small bowl. Add to the flour mixture and beat until smooth, scraping down sides of bowl once or twice.

Spread the batter into the prepared baking pan and sprinkle with the reserved topping.

Bake 30 to 35 minutes or until golden brown and a toothpick inserted in center comes out clean. Cool slightly on wire cooling rack and cut into squares to serve. Serve warm.

> SECRETS TO SUCCESS: Cutting the cold butter into ½-inch cubes makes it easier to combine into crumbs.

CHOCOLATE SWIRL COFFEE CAKE

The high butter and sugar content of this coffee cake results in such a tender cake that you could even serve it for dessert. The mini chocolate chips carry the chocolate flavor into every bite, and the unsweetened cocoa creates chocolate stripes throughout.

MAKES 12 TO 16 SERVINGS

FILLING

3 tablespoons firmly packed brown sugar
1 tablespoon unsweetened cocoa
1 tablespoon butter

CAKE

2 cups all-purpose flour
1 teaspoon baking powder
1 teaspoon baking soda
¼ teaspoon salt
¾ cup butter, softened
1½ cups sugar
1 cup sour cream
1 teaspoon vanilla
2 eggs, beaten
½ cup semisweet chocolate mini chips
Powdered sugar
Unsweetened cocoa

Heat oven to 350°F with oven rack in middle. Spray a nonstick 10-cup Bundt pan generously with nonstick cooking spray.

FILLING

Mix brown sugar and cocoa in a small bowl and cut in butter until mixture resembles coarse crumbs with some pea-sized pieces. Reserve filling.

CAKE

Combine flour, baking powder, baking soda, and salt in a medium bowl.

Beat butter and sugar in bowl of a heavy-duty mixer on Medium speed until creamy, scraping down bowl once or twice. Add sour cream, vanilla, and eggs and beat until smooth. Scrape down sides of bowl.

Reduce mixer speed to Low, add the flour mixture, and beat just until the flour disappears. Stir in chocolate chips.

Spoon half of the batter into prepared pan and sprinkle with filling. Cover with remaining batter, spreading evenly to cover the filling. Keep filling away from sides of pan to prevent sticking.

Bake 35 to 50 minutes or until a toothpick inserted in center comes out clean. Cool 10 minutes on wire cooling rack. Remove cake from pan (see Baker's Notes below) and cool completely. Sprinkle a little powdered sugar and cocoa over coffee cake.

BAKER'S NOTES: Spray the Bundt pan generously with nonstick cooking spray or grease with vegetable shortening and coat with flour. Make sure the ridges are coated so the cake will come out completely.

Use a metal spatula to release the center and loosen the sides of the cake from the pan. With the cake side up, gently shake the pan to loosen the bottom, rotating as you shake. If it doesn't release, use the spatula to lift from the bottom. Carefully remove the cake from the pan by inverting it onto a cooling rack.

SECRETS TO SUCCESS: Don't use regular-size semisweet chocolate chips because they will sink to the bottom of the cake.

Use a mesh strainer or a tea infuser to sprinkle the powdered sugar and cocoa.

It takes a little practice to remove a Bundt cake from the pan, but if it doesn't come out completely, just slice and arrange the slices on a serving plate.

apple praline coffee cake

When you prepare this coffee cake for a special occasion, arrange small pecan halves instead of chopped pecans on top to dress it up. Apples and brown sugar keep this cake moist for several days.

MAKES 12 TO 16 SERVINGS

1½ cups chopped peeled apples (about 2 medium)
⅓ cup sugar
2 teaspoons cinnamon, divided
3 cups all-purpose flour
3 teaspoons baking powder
½ teaspoon salt
1 cup butter, softened
1 cup sugar
2 eggs, beaten
1 teaspoon vanilla
1 cup milk

GLAZE

¼ cup firmly packed brown sugar
¼ cup butter
1 cup powdered sugar, sifted
2 tablespoons whipping cream or milk
½ cup chopped pecans

Heat oven to 375°F with oven rack in middle. Spray a nonstick 10-cup Bundt pan with nonstick spray or thoroughly grease and flour.

Combine apples, sugar, and 1 teaspoon cinnamon in medium bowl. Combine flour, baking powder, remaining 1 teaspoon cinnamon, and salt in another medium bowl.

Beat butter in bowl of a heavy-duty mixer on Medium speed until creamy, scraping down sides of bowl once or twice. Gradually add sugar and continue beating until light in color. Scrape down sides of bowl. Beat in eggs and vanilla.

Reduce mixer speed to Low and add the flour mixture in three additions, alternating with two additions of milk. Scrape down bowl after each addition. Beat until smooth.

By hand, stir in the apple mixture. Spoon the batter into prepared pan, and spread evenly with a metal spatula.

Bake 45 to 60 minutes or until a toothpick inserted in center comes out clean. The apples should be fork-tender. Cool on wire cooling rack 15 minutes and remove cake from pan (see Baker's Notes below).

GLAZE

Heat brown sugar and ¼ cup butter in small saucepan over medium heat, bringing mixture to a boil while stirring constantly. Reduce heat to low and cook until butter is absorbed, about 1 minute. Remove from heat and add whipping cream and powdered sugar. Beat until smooth.

Drizzle glaze over cake, allowing some to run down the sides. Sprinkle with pecans.

BAKER'S NOTES: Spray the Bundt pan generously with nonstick cooking spray or grease with shortening and coat with flour. Make sure the ridges are coated so the cake will come out completely.

Use a metal spatula to release the center and loosen the sides of the cake from the pan. With the cake side up, gently shake the pan to loosen the bottom, rotating as you shake. Carefully remove the cake from the pan by inverting it onto a cooling rack.

Because the glaze is cooked, it sets up quickly. As soon as it is smooth, drizzle it over the cake.

SECRETS TO SUCCESS: Use an electric knife or a serrated knife for easier slicing.

Place a piece of waxed paper or a cookie sheet under the cooling rack for easy clean-up after glazing.

CHERRY BRUNCH CAKE

Cherries are one of my favorite fruits, and every summer we bake cherry pies using the cherries from the two cherry trees in our back yard. During the rest of the year, dried cherries capture that sharp cherry flavor that makes your mouth pucker and is then followed by a burst of sweetness.

MAKES 8 TO 10 SERVINGS

2 cups all-purpose flour

1 ½ teaspoons baking powder

½ teaspoon baking soda

¼ teaspoon salt

½ cup butter, softened

1 cup sugar

1 egg

1 teaspoon almond extract

½ teaspoon vanilla

½ cup lowfat buttermilk

½ cup coarsely chopped dried cherries

GLAZE

1 cup powdered sugar

4–5 tablespoons whipping cream or milk

½ teaspoon almond extract

⅓ cup sliced almonds, toasted

Heat oven to 350°F with oven rack in middle. Lightly grease bottom and ½ inch up sides of a 9-inch springform pan.

Combine flour, baking powder, baking soda, and salt in a medium bowl.

Beat butter and sugar in bowl of a heavy-duty mixer on Medium speed until creamy, scraping down bowl once or twice. Add egg, almond extract, and vanilla and beat until smooth. Reduce mixer speed to Low and beat in buttermilk.

Beat in the flour mixture, scrape down sides of bowl, and beat until smooth. By hand, stir in the cherries. Pour batter into the prepared pan.

Bake 35 to 40 minutes or until golden brown and a toothpick inserted in center comes out clean. The cake may be pulling away from pan sides. Cool 15 minutes on wire cooling rack. Run a spatula around cake to loosen it from pan sides. Release the sides of springform pan (do not remove the pan's bottom) and remove cake.

GLAZE

Beat powdered sugar, whipping cream, and almond extract in small bowl until smooth. Spread glaze over cake, allowing it to drip over sides. Sprinkle with almonds. Serve warm or at room temperature.

BAKER'S NOTES: Toast almonds in oven at 350°F for 5 to 7 minutes. Watch almonds because they burn easily. They will continue to darken a little after they are removed from the oven. Cool.

You can make buttermilk by adding ½ teaspoon of lemon juice to ½ of cup milk.

SECRETS TO SUCCESS: Add whipping cream to the glaze until it is thin enough to drip over the sides of the cake.

SOUR CREAM BREAKFAST BREAD

Everybody recognizes this tender and cake-like quick bread that is rich in butter and crunchy with pecans. Originally, the directions for this coffee cake called for sprinkling the filling in three layers not two, but I think it's easier to make only two layers. Keep the filling away from the sides of the pan so the bread will be easier to remove.

MAKES 1 LOAF (10 to 12 slices)

FILLING

⅓ cup sugar

⅓ cup finely chopped pecans

1 teaspoon cinnamon

BREAD

2 cups all-purpose flour

1 teaspoon baking powder

½ teaspoon baking soda

⅛ teaspoon salt

¾ cup butter, softened

1½ cups sugar

2 eggs

1 teaspoon vanilla

1 cup sour cream

Heat oven to 350°F with oven rack in middle. Spray a 9 x 5-inch loaf pan with nonstick cooking spray, or thoroughly grease and flour.

FILLING

Mix sugar, pecans, and cinnamon in a small bowl and reserve.

BReaD

Combine flour, baking powder, baking soda, and salt in medium bowl.

Beat butter and sugar in bowl of a heavy-duty mixer on Medium speed until creamy, scraping down sides of bowl once or twice. Add eggs and vanilla and beat until smooth. Reduce mixer speed to Low and beat in sour cream. Add the flour mixture and beat until smooth.

Pour about half the batter into prepared loaf pan and sprinkle about half of the filling over it. Using a small metal spatula, swirl the filling lightly into the batter.

Top with the remaining batter and sprinkle with remaining filling.

Bake 45 to 55 minutes or until a toothpick inserted in center comes out clean. The bread will also be pulling away from sides of pan.

Cool 10 minutes on wire cooling rack. Loosen bread from sides of pan and lift gently to loosen and release it from pan bottom. Place rack over bread and invert it. Turn bread top side up and cool thoroughly. This bread slices better the second day.

BAKER'S NOTES: After filling the pan, I thump it once or twice on the counter to eliminate large pockets of air.

I have prepared this many times with reduced-fat sour cream, but I never use anything but real butter.

SECRETS TO SUCCESS: Use an electric knife for easy slicing.

RaspBeRRy cReam cHeese coffee cake

There's a bakery in Lawrence, Kansas, that makes a tart similar to this cake with a sweet cream cheese filling and cherry preserves. I prefer seedless raspberry jam and have added almond paste for its delicate flavor and slightly chewy texture.

MAKES 8 SERVINGS

1½ cups all-purpose flour
¾ cup sugar, divided
1 teaspoon baking powder
¼ teaspoon baking soda
¼ teaspoon salt
½ cup butter
¼ cup milk
1 teaspoon almond extract
2 eggs, divided
1 (8-ounce) package cream cheese, softened
½ cup crumbled almond paste, from a 7-ounce package
⅓ cup seedless raspberry jam

ICING

½ cup powdered sugar
4–5 teaspoons milk
½ teaspoon almond extract

Heat oven to 350°F with oven rack in middle. Grease and flour bottom and sides of a 9-inch springform pan.

Combine flour, ½ cup sugar, baking powder, baking soda, and salt in large bowl. Cut in butter with a pastry blender until mixture resembles coarse crumbs with some pea-sized pieces.

Combine milk, almond extract, and 1 egg in a small bowl and beat until smooth. Add liquid mixture to flour mixture, and stir until evenly moistened. Spread batter on bottom and about ¾ inch up sides of the springform pan.

Beat cream cheese, remaining ¼ cup sugar, and remaining egg in bowl of heavy-duty mixer on Medium speed until smooth. Add crumbled almond paste and beat well. Pour filling into center of cake batter.

Drop raspberry jam over the cream cheese mixture in large spoonfuls and swirl lightly.

Bake 34 to 38 minutes or until cream cheese is set and cake is lightly browned. Cool slightly on wire cooling rack.

ICING

Combine powdered sugar, almond extract, and milk in small bowl and beat until smooth. Drizzle over coffee cake.

Cool coffee cake completely or serve warm. Run a spatula around the edge of the pan and remove the sides of the springform. Do not remove the bottom of the pan. Store any remaining cake in refrigerator.

BAKER'S NOTE: Spreading the cake batter up the sides of the springform pan provides a base for the filling and makes it easier to remove the sides of the springform pan.

SECRETS TO SUCCESS: Almond paste can be found in the baking section of most supermarkets near the fruit fillings. If the almond paste is dry and firm, I either chop it in a food processor until it is coarsely ground or grate it with a grater.

chapter four

BROWNIES AND BARS

THINK OF A PAN OF BARS as a giant cookie and a pan of brownies as the best cookie of all.

After baking, bars are usually cooled in the pan before cutting. Requiring the slightest amount of effort, a pan of bars yields many servings. Because they usually are moist and sturdy and generally keep well, bars and brownies are excellent to send as gifts. Most should be stored at room temperature, unless the filling contains eggs, as in the recipe for Sunny Citrus Bars, and needs to be refrigerated.

Most bars need only pantry staples such as sugar, flour, butter, and eggs. I use butter for bars, but margarine is an acceptable substitute. Be sure nuts from the pantry are not past their freshness date because nuts are high in fat and can turn rancid and ruin the flavor of the bars.

Bars usually are made in a 13 x 9-inch baking pan and can include a crisp bottom crust with a wide variety of toppings or fillings. Layered or filled, chewy or crisp— the choices are endless.

Brownies are also bars, dark and fudgy and dense with chocolate flavor and with a crinkled top. I think brownies have the best flavor when two kinds of chocolate are combined—semisweet and unsweetened. The semisweet glaze adds depth to the rich chocolate flavor. Using melted butter instead of creaming the butter with sugar leads to a fudgier brownie. Brownies are usually baked in a 13 x 9-inch baking pan.

Baking bars and brownies in the proper size pan, which contains the right amount of batter, results in even doneness. I often line a 13 x 9-inch baking pan with aluminum foil, extending the foil a few inches on both of the long sides. After cooling on wire cooling racks, the entire recipe can be removed before cutting, making that process easier. When cutting bars or brownies still in the pan, it helps to remove the corner piece first so the rest of them will come out more easily.

Store most bars and brownies at room temperature; they keep well and should be stored tightly covered. For longer storage, wrap tightly and freeze. Thaw at room temperature—it only takes a few minutes. When storing bars and brownies, separate strong-flavored bars and store in different containers. A piece of parchment or waxed paper placed between the layers prevents them from sticking together. Bars with a custardy filling, like Sunny Citrus Bars, should be refrigerated.

Always use real chocolate—the best you can afford—not an inexpensive version. Unsweetened baking chocolate has the highest amount of chocolate liquor, which is what gives chocolate its flavor. Experiment with dark bittersweet chocolate and semisweet chocolate—bittersweet often has more chocolate liquor. There are many kinds of chocolate and many manufacturers, so it's important to choose wisely.

I melt chocolate in a double boiler over simmering water (see How to Melt Chocolate, page 12). I start melting the chocolate before I get the other ingredients together, and it's usually melted before I need it. Chocolate will burn, which is why it is safer to melt it on the stove, than in the microwave. Be careful not to get any water into the chocolate or it will turn into hard lumps.

Many bars are easy to assemble by hand, especially brownies, but for others it's easier with an electric mixer. A hand mixer works as well as a heavy-duty mixer here. Although most bars are baked in 13 x 9-inch baking pan, it's good to have a 9 x 9-inch pan and a 15 x 10 x 1-inch jelly roll pan.

FabuLous FuDGY BROWNIes

"These brownies are really good," my daughter commented as she went back for seconds. Unlike brownies from a box, they have a fudgy, deep chocolate flavor and moist, dense texture, and they can be prepared almost as quickly. Omit the glaze if you like, but that's what sets homemade apart.

MAKES 36 BROWNIES

½ cup butter
5 ounces unsweetened chocolate, coarsely chopped
2 cups sugar
1 teaspoon vanilla
4 eggs, beaten
1 cup flour

GLaZe

4 ounces semisweet chocolate, coarsely chopped
¼ cup butter

Place butter and chocolate in a medium bowl and set bowl over, not in, simmering water until chocolate melts; or use a double boiler. The last little lumps will melt as mixture sits. Cool slightly.

Heat oven to 350°F with oven rack in middle. Line bottom of a 13 x 9-inch baking pan with aluminum foil, extending foil about 2 inches beyond pan on each long side. Spray lightly with nonstick cooking spray.

Combine sugar, vanilla, and melted chocolate in a large bowl, and stir slowly to mix. Add eggs and mix with a wire whisk until well blended. Slowly stir in flour until it disappears. Whisk about 15 seconds or until smooth. Pour into prepared pan, pushing batter into the corners.

Bake 20 to 25 minutes until center seems set when touched lightly with a finger. Brownies will also start to pull away from pan edges. When set in center, the batter won't jiggle. Cool in pan on wire cooling rack.

GLAZE

Melt butter and semisweet chocolate in a small bowl set over, not in, simmering water, stirring occasionally. Cool until slightly thickened.

Pour glaze over brownies and spread evenly. Let stand until glaze is set.

Remove brownies intact from pan by loosening ends with a metal spatula and lifting, using the aluminum foil. Cut into bars. Make sure foil is not stuck on bottom of any brownies.

> BAKER'S NOTES: Because I have found that semisweet chocolate chips do not melt as smoothly as baking squares, I recommend using the squares for a smooth glaze.
>
> SECRETS TO SUCCESS: I like to line the pan with foil because it makes the brownies easy to remove and cut into perfect squares.

zebra Brownie squares

These brownies were awarded first place when my daughter entered them in an office contest. Be sure to purchase a box of brownie mix that makes a 13 x 9-inch pan of brownies. Chocolate chip cookie dough is my family's favorite, but you can use any flavor dough. Swirl the cookie dough into the batter so it isn't just sitting on top. I named these "Zebra Brownies" because of the black and white stripes on top.

MAKES 24 BROWNIES

1 package (1 pound 3.8 ounces) brownie mix (you will likely need 2 eggs, water, and vegetable oil)
½ of 18-ounce package refrigerated chocolate chip cookie dough
1 container white chocolate or vanilla frosting
1 cup powdered sugar
3 tablespoons unsweetened cocoa
2 tablespoons butter, melted
2 tablespoons milk
½ teaspoon vanilla

Heat oven to 350°F with oven rack in middle. Line bottom of a 13 x 9-inch baking pan with aluminum foil, extending foil about 2 inches beyond pan on each long side. Spray lightly with nonstick cooking spray.

Prepare brownies as directed on box for fudgy brownies. (You will need eggs, water, and vegetable oil.) Pour batter into prepared pan and spread evenly.

Crumble cookie dough over the brownie batter. Using a metal spatula, swirl brownie batter around and through the cookie dough.

Bake 25 to 30 minutes or until center seems set when touched lightly with a finger. Brownies will also start to pull away from pan edges. Cool in pan, on wire cooling rack.

Spread cooled brownies with white chocolate frosting.

Sift powdered sugar and unsweetened cocoa into a small bowl. Add butter, milk, and vanilla and stir until smooth. Scrape down sides of bowl once or twice. Add a little more milk if frosting is too thick for drizzling.

Place chocolate frosting in a resealable food storage bag. Snip off a corner of the bag, and drizzle chocolate over the white frosting, creating zebra stripes.

Remove brownies intact from the pan by loosening ends with a metal spatula and lifting, using the aluminum foil. Cut into 24 squares. Make sure foil is not stuck on bottom of any brownies.

BAKER'S NOTES: Soften the cookie dough slightly at room temperature so that it is easier to crumble.

If the cookie dough is very sticky, spray your fingers with nonstick cooking spray while crumbling it.

espresso Brownies

The coffee flavor softens the richness of these dense squares covered with a fudgy frosting, and they're perfect with hot espresso. I usually cut these brownies into 48 bars because they are so rich. Sprinkle the brownies with powdered sugar if you don't want to make the frosting.

MAKES 48 BROWNIES

½ cup butter
4 ounces unsweetened chocolate, coarsely chopped
2 tablespoons warm, strong coffee
1 teaspoon instant espresso powder, if desired
2 cups sugar
1 teaspoon vanilla
4 eggs, beaten
1 ¼ cups all-purpose flour
1 cup chopped walnuts

FROSTING

1 ½ cups powdered sugar
2 tablespoons unsweetened cocoa
Pinch of salt
¼ cup butter, melted
2 tablespoons strong coffee
½ teaspoon vanilla

Place butter and chocolate in a medium bowl and set bowl over, not in, simmering water until chocolate melts; or use a double boiler. Remove from heat. The last little lumps will melt as the mixture sits. Cool slightly.

Heat oven to 350°F with oven rack in middle. Spray bottom of a 13 x 9-inch baking pan with nonstick cooking spray.

Combine coffee and instant espresso in a small bowl, and stir until espresso dissolves. Stir into the chocolate mixture.

Combine sugar, vanilla, and eggs in a medium bowl. Whisk until smooth. Add chocolate mixture, and stir slowly with a spoon until uniformly mixed. Add flour and stir slowly until it disappears, then whisk about 30 seconds until smooth. Stir in walnuts.

Pour batter into prepared pan, pushing it into corners with a small spatula. Smooth the top.

Bake 19 to 24 minutes until center seems set when touched lightly with a finger. Brownies will also start to pull away from pan edges. When set in the center, the batter won't jiggle. Cool in pan, on wire cooling rack.

FROSTING

Sift powdered sugar, cocoa, and salt together in a medium bowl. Add butter, coffee, and vanilla and beat with wire whisk until smooth. Spread frosting onto brownies with an offset spatula. Because the butter is melted, the frosting will set up as it cools. Cut into bars.

> BAKER'S NOTE: Instant espresso powder is usually available at supermarkets. If it's unavailable, use double strength coffee.

BUTTERSCOTCH CASHEW BLONDIES

The opposite of a brownie is a blondie—the colors are different but the texture of the bars is similar. It is much easier to determine doneness in the blondies than in the brownies. If the blondies are not done, you can see the batter move under the top crust when you shake the pan. Because of the high amount of sugar in these bars, the edges rise and get dark and chewy—I think this is the best part!

MAKES 36 BARS

2 cups all-purpose flour
2 teaspoons baking powder
½ teaspoon baking soda
½ teaspoon salt
2 cups firmly packed brown sugar
1 cup butter, melted
2 teaspoons vanilla
2 eggs, beaten
1 cup butterscotch chips (6 ounces)
1 cup cashew halves and pieces, coarsely chopped

Heat oven to 350°F with oven rack in middle. Line bottom of a 13 x 9-inch baking pan with aluminum foil, extending foil about 2 inches beyond pan on each long side. Spray lightly with nonstick cooking spray.

Combine flour, baking powder, baking soda, and salt in a medium bowl.

Combine brown sugar, butter, and vanilla in a large bowl and stir slowly to mix. Add eggs and mix with a wire whisk until well blended. Slowly stir in flour mixture until it is moistened. Beat with wire whisk 30 seconds until smooth.

Add butterscotch chips and cashews. Pour batter into prepared pan and spread evenly.

Bake 30 to 35 minutes or until center seems set when touched lightly with a finger. The blondies will also start to pull away from pan edges. When checking, shake the pan a little and see if batter jiggles. A toothpick will come out dry. Cool in pan on wire cooling rack.

Remove blondies intact from pan by loosening ends with a metal spatula and lifting out, using the aluminum foil. Cut into bars. Make sure foil is not stuck on bottom of any blondies.

BAKER'S NOTE: When you combine the brown sugar, butter, eggs, and vanilla, mix until smooth, crushing any lumps of brown sugar.

apple blondies

I always make these bars in the fall when apples are harvested. Every part of the country has local varieties of apples so try some local apples and find a favorite for cooking. These are moist bars that keep well, especially when they are frosted.

MAKES 24 BARS

1 ½ cups all-purpose flour
1 teaspoon baking powder
1 teaspoon cinnamon
½ teaspoon baking soda
¼ teaspoon salt
½ cup butter, melted
1 cup firmly packed brown sugar
2 eggs, beaten
1 teaspoon vanilla
½ cup chopped peeled apple (1 small)
Buttercream Frosting (see page 280)

Heat oven to 350°F with oven rack in middle. Spray bottom of a 9 x 9-inch baking pan with nonstick baking spray.

Combine flour, baking powder, cinnamon, baking soda, and salt in a medium bowl.

Mix butter and brown sugar in a large bowl and beat in the eggs and vanilla. Slowly stir in flour mixture until flour disappears. Beat with a wire whisk 15 seconds until smooth. Stir in apple and spread into prepared pan.

Bake 25 to 30 minutes or until center seems set when touched lightly with a finger. The blondies will also start to pull away from pan edges. When checking doneness, shake pan a little to see if batter jiggles. A toothpick will come out dry. Cool on a wire cooling rack.

When completely cool, spread with Buttercream Frosting and cut into bars.

BAKER'S NOTE: I often use Golden Delicious apples because they are available year round. Chop the apples into small pieces that are easy to distribute in the batter.

SECRETS TO SUCCESS: After the flour is added, this dough is very stiff, but it is still important to mix well.

BROWNIES ALASKA WITH HAZELNUT SAUCE

Coffee ice cream hides under a snowy mountain of meringue and sits on a fudgy brownie in my version of Baked Alaska. This spectacular dessert is surprisingly easy to prepare. The key to success is freezing the assembled dessert thoroughly before baking briefly in a very hot oven.

MAKES 4 SERVINGS

> 1 package brownie mix (for 8- or 9-inch pan)
> 2 cups coffee ice cream, softened
> 3 egg whites, room temperature
> ¼ teaspoon cream of tartar
> ⅔ cup sugar

HazeLnuT sauce

        ½ cup firmly packed brown sugar
        ½ cup light corn syrup
        ¼ cup butter
        ½ cup chopped toasted hazelnuts (also called filberts)
         1 tablespoon hazelnut liqueur, if desired
         1 teaspoon vanilla

Line an 8- or 9-inch square cake pan with aluminum foil or parchment paper, extending foil 2 inches beyond two opposite sides of pan. Prepare brownies as directed on package. Bake as directed, and cool completely on a wire rack.

Loosen edges of brownies and remove from pan by lifting with the foil. Cut 4 circles out of brownies, using 2½ to 3¼-inch biscuit cutter. Be sure the aluminum foil underneath brownies is removed.

Choose a cookie sheet or pan that will fit in your freezer, and line it with aluminum foil. Place the round brownies on the foil and top each with ½-cup scoop of ice cream. Freeze uncovered about 2 hours or until firm.

Place egg whites in bowl of a heavy-duty mixer fitted with the whisk. Add cream of tartar and beat on Medium speed until foamy. Increase mixer speed to High, and beat until soft peaks form.

Gradually add the sugar, 1 tablespoon at a time, while beating on High, scraping down sides of bowl occasionally. After sugar is added, beat until stiff glossy peaks are formed when whisk is lifted.

Spread the meringue over ice cream and brownies with small spatula, covering them completely and spreading to edges to seal. Cover lightly and freeze until serving. Nonstick aluminum foil works well for covering. Shape it gently around desserts.

HazeLnuT sauce

Combine brown sugar, corn syrup, and butter in small saucepan. Bring to a boil over medium heat, stirring constantly. Boil 1 minute. Remove from heat and stir in hazelnuts, liqueur, and vanilla. Store sauce at room temperature.

The meringue-covered brownies should be frozen overnight before baking. Heat oven to 450°F with oven rack in middle. Bake 2 to 3 minutes or until meringue is lightly browned—watch constantly.

Heat sauce to lukewarm and pour a little onto individual serving dishes. Top with the Brownies Alaska. Everyone, including you, will be impressed!

BAKER'S NOTES: Hazelnut liqueur is called Frangelico and has a unique flavor, but you can also use an almond or coffee flavored liqueur.

To determine if the sugar is dissolved, rub a little meringue between your finger and thumb. It will feel gritty if the sugar is not dissolved and the whites need to be beaten longer.

SECRET TO SUCCESS: You can purchase chopped hazelnuts (also called filberts); but if you buy the whole nuts, the outer skin, which is bitter, should be removed.

An empty tuna can or a drinking glass can be used as a guide if you don't have a biscuit cutter. A wooden cutting board can be placed under the baking sheet to serve as an insulator when you are browning the meringue.

TOFFEE BARS

These bars are great to make at the last minute—most of the ingredients are already in your kitchen. I keep a bag of toffee bits on hand for emergencies! Toffee bits are found in the baking section of supermarkets, near the chocolate chips. Or you can crush chocolate-covered toffee bars.

MAKES 30 BARS

2 cups all-purpose flour
2 teaspoons baking powder
¼ teaspoon salt
2 cups firmly packed brown sugar
½ cup butter, melted
2 eggs, beaten
1 teaspoon vanilla
1 cup butterscotch chips
⅔ cup toffee bits
1 cup semisweet chocolate chips

Heat oven to 350°F with oven rack in middle. Spray bottom of a 13 x 9-inch baking pan with nonstick cooking spray.

Combine flour, baking powder, and salt in a medium bowl.

Mix brown sugar and butter in a large bowl. Add eggs and vanilla and beat until smooth. Slowly stir in the flour mixture until it is evenly moistened. Beat with a whisk until batter is smooth. Stir in butterscotch chips and toffee bits. Scrape into pan and spread evenly.

Bake 26 to 30 minutes or until golden brown and set in the center. Sprinkle with chocolate chips. Let stand 3 minutes or until chocolate melts and spread evenly. Cool completely on wire cooling rack.

> BAKER'S NOTE: You can crush chocolate-covered toffee bars in a food storage bag with a rolling pin.

CHOCOLATE CHEESECAKE BARS

Chocolate and cheesecake are combined here—what could be better? These easy bars keep well in the refrigerator several days. The bittersweet chocolate drizzle makes a perfect finishing touch.

MAKES 24 TO 30 BARS

> 8 ounces semisweet chocolate, coarsely chopped
> 1 ounce bittersweet chocolate, coarsely chopped
> 1 ½ cups all-purpose flour
> ½ cup firmly packed brown sugar
> ½ cup cold butter
> 2 (8-ounce) packages cream cheese, softened
> ⅔ cup sugar
> 2 eggs
> ½ cup whipping cream
> 2 teaspoons vanilla

Melt semisweet chocolate in a small bowl, set over, not in, simmering water, stirring occasionally. The last little lumps will melt as mixture sits. Cool slightly.

Place bittersweet chocolate in a small dish, and set over hot water off the heat.

Heat oven to 350°F with oven rack in middle. Lightly spray bottom and about ½ inch up sides of a 13 x 9-inch baking pan.

Mix flour and brown sugar in a medium bowl. Cut in cold butter with a pastry blender until mixture resembles coarse crumbs with some pea-sized pieces.

Press crust evenly into bottom of prepared pan. Using your fingers, press crust slightly up sides of pan. Bake 8 minutes or until edges begin to brown.

Beat cream cheese in bowl of heavy-duty mixer on Medium speed until creamy. Scrape down sides of bowl and gradually add sugar. Add eggs, one at a time, beating after each addition. Scrape down sides of bowl, and beat in whipping cream and vanilla.

Add melted semisweet chocolate and beat until mixed. Pour filling into the partially baked crust and spread evenly. Drizzle with melted bittersweet chocolate.

Bake 23 to 28 minutes or until center is set and does not jiggle. Cool on cooling rack. Refrigerate about 4 hours until chilled. Cut into bars and store in refrigerator.

BAKER'S NOTE: Use squares of chocolate, not chocolate chips, because the squares melt smoothly.

SECRETS TO SUCCESS: I have a glass 13 x 9-inch baking dish that I use for these bars. After the bars are cooled, I cover them with the dish's plastic lid and refrigerate.

SCOTTISH SHORTBREAD

Shortbread is the most basic cookie—made only of flour, sugar, and butter. Traditionally, the dough was pressed into a circle and cut into wedges before baking, but I like to cut it into bars because they are smaller and easier to eat.

MAKES 3 ½ TO 4 DOZEN BARS

> 4 cups all-purpose flour
> 1 cup powdered sugar
> 2 cups unsalted butter

GARNISH, IF DESIRED

> 2 ounces bittersweet or semisweet, chocolate
> 1 teaspoon solid vegetable shortening

Heat oven to 350°F with oven rack in middle.

Beat flour, sugar, and butter in bowl of a heavy-duty mixer on Medium speed until crumbly and evenly mixed, scraping down sides of bowl once or twice.

Press dough, about ⅜ inch thick, into an ungreased 15 x 10 x 1-inch baking pan. The dough will not fill the whole pan. I usually press to fill the width and about ¾ of the length. Cut into 3 x 1-inch bars, using a pizza wheel. Prick well with a fork.

Bake 20 to 25 minutes or until edges are just beginning to brown. Classic shortbread is very pale. While bars are still warm, cut again. After cutting, the bars can cool in pan on wire cooling rack.

GARNISH

Melt butter and chocolate in a medium bowl set over, not in, simmering water, or use a double boiler. Using a fork, drizzle chocolate over shortbread. When chocolate is set, remove the shortbread from pan.

Store loosely covered at room temperature. Do not refrigerate or the chocolate will loose its gloss.

> BAKER'S NOTE: Melting the chocolate with shortening thins it so it can be drizzled. Using a fork, drizzle the melted chocolate in every direction.
>
> SECRETS TO SUCCESS: I use unsalted butter in this recipe because its cultured flavor is present in every bite.

sunny CITRUS BaRS

Here's my favorite lemon bar recipe. I use orange juice, in addition to lemon juice, to balance the sharpness of the lemon juice. I am a tea drinker, and I think hot tea in a delicate china cup—or a tall glass of iced tea—served with lemon bars is the perfect refreshment.

MAKES 36 BARS

CRUST

2 cups all-purpose flour
1 cup powdered sugar
¾ cup butter

FILLING

1½ cups sugar
3 tablespoons all-purpose flour
1 teaspoon baking powder
⅛ teaspoon salt
4 eggs, beaten

½ cup freshly squeezed lemon juice (1–2 lemons)
¼ cup freshly squeezed orange juice (1 orange)
¼ cup butter, melted
1 teaspoon grated lemon peel
1 teaspoon grated orange peel

GLaZe

1 ½ cups powdered sugar
2–4 tablespoons orange juice

Heat oven to 350°F with oven rack in middle. Lightly spray bottom of a 13 x 9-inch baking pan with nonstick cooking spray.

CRUST

Mix flour and powdered sugar in a medium bowl. Cut in butter with a pastry blender until mixture resembles coarse crumbs with some pea-sized pieces. Press crust evenly in bottom and slightly up sides of baking pan.

Bake 20 to 25 minutes or until the edges begin to brown. Reduce oven temperature to 325°F.

FILLInG

Combine sugar, flour, baking powder, and salt in a medium bowl. Beat in eggs using wire whisk. When smooth, stir in lemon juice, orange juice, butter, lemon peel, and orange peel and mix well. Pour over the hot crust.

Bake 25 to 30 minutes or until filling is set in the center and a knife comes out clean, although it will still be wet. Cool on wire cooling rack to room temperature.

GLAZE

Combine powdered sugar and 2 tablespoons orange juice in a small bowl and beat with a small whisk until smooth. Spread glaze over cooled bars. Store bars in refrigerator.

BAKER'S NOTES: When you press the crust mixture between your fingers, you shouldn't feel large, cold lumps of butter.

Sift the powdered sugar for a smooth glaze.

SECRETS TO SUCCESS: To grate the lemon and orange peel, I use my microplane grater. I consider it a kitchen essential. It makes it easy to grate the peel of citrus fruit without including the bitter white layer beneath it. Always grate the peel before squeezing juice.

CHEWY CHERRY SQUARES

While living in Florida, my mom got this recipe from a Canadian friend. I especially like the chewy coconut and nut topping with cherry preserves, but you can use seedless raspberry jam or strawberry jam. When I'm asked to bring bars, I often bring these because everybody else usually brings brownies.

MAKES 25 SQUARES

CRUST

　　　1 ½ cups all-purpose flour
　　　⅓ cup firmly packed brown sugar
　　　⅓ cup butter
　　　⅓ cup cherry preserves

TOPPING

>1 cup firmly packed brown sugar
>
>2 tablespoons butter, softened
>
>1 teaspoon vanilla
>
>1 egg
>
>1 cup flaked sweetened coconut
>
>1 cup chopped pecans

Heat oven to 350°F with oven rack in middle. Spray bottom of a 9 x 9-inch baking pan with nonstick cooking spray.

CRUST

Mix flour and brown sugar in a medium bowl. Cut in butter with a pastry blender until mixture resembles coarse crumbs with some pea-sized pieces. Press crust evenly in bottom and slightly up sides of pan.

Bake 10 minutes or until edges begin to brown. Spread preserves over the warm crust.

TOPPING

Beat brown sugar, butter, and vanilla in bowl of a heavy-duty mixer on Medium speed until smooth, scraping down sides of bowl once or twice.

Add egg and mix well. Stir in coconut and pecans. Drop topping over the preserves, leaving some preserves uncovered.

Bake 23 to 28 minutes or until topping is browned. Cool on wire cooling rack. Cut into squares.

BAKER'S NOTE: You can bake these square bars in an 8 x 8-inch baking pan. The baking time remains the same.

TURTLE BARS

Since the yummy topping for these bars comes from melted caramels, make this first because it takes a little time to unwrap the caramels. You can use caramel sauce, but it's just not the same. To save time, buy graham cracker crumbs rather than crushing your own.

MAKES 24 BARS

30 caramels, unwrapped
¼ cup milk
⅔ cup firmly packed brown sugar
½ cup butter, softened
½ teaspoon vanilla
1 egg
2½ cups graham cracker crumbs
⅓ cup all-purpose flour
⅛ teaspoon salt
1 cup milk chocolate chunks (6 ounces)
1 cup pecan halves

Heat oven to 350°F with oven rack in middle. Line bottom of a 13 x 9-inch baking pan with aluminum foil, extending foil about 2 inches beyond long sides of pan. Spray lightly with nonstick cooking spray.

Melt caramels with milk in a small saucepan over low heat, stirring often, until smooth. Cool slightly.

Beat brown sugar, butter, vanilla, and egg in bowl of a heavy-duty mixer on Medium speed until smooth, scraping down sides of bowl once or twice. Add graham cracker crumbs, flour, and salt. Mix until crumbly on Low speed.

Remove 1 ½ cups of mixture and set aside. Press remaining crumb mixture into bottom of prepared baking pan.

Sprinkle chocolate chunks and pecans evenly over crust. Pour melted caramels over top. Crumble the reserved graham cracker mixture unevenly over the caramel sauce, leaving some of the filling uncovered.

Bake 20 to 25 minutes or until caramel mixture is bubbling and edges of crust are beginning to brown. Cool completely on wire cooling rack. Remove in one piece from pan by loosening the ends with a metal spatula and lifting, using the aluminum foil. Cut into bars.

BAKER'S NOTE: The graham cracker mixture is very sticky and must be spread evenly, so I usually spray my fingers with nonstick cooking spray before pressing out the crust.

SECRETS TO SUCCESS: You can use semisweet, bittersweet, or milk chocolate chunks, but I prefer milk chocolate. Chop the pecan halves if they are large and the bars will be easier to cut.

Banana Bars with Brown Sugar Frosting

My husband eats a banana every day, but sometimes we have too many ripe ones. Needless to say, I bake a lot of banana bars and banana bread! When the bananas are very ripe, I don't bother to mash them but simply cut them into chunks, add them to the batter, and let the mixer do its job.

MAKES 36 BARS

2 cups all-purpose flour
1 teaspoon baking soda
½ teaspoon salt
½ cup butter, softened
1½ cups sugar
½ cup sour cream
1 teaspoon vanilla
2 eggs
1 cup mashed ripe bananas (2 medium)
1 cup chopped walnuts

FROSTING

½ cup firmly packed brown sugar
¼ cup butter
¼ cup whipping cream or milk
1 teaspoon vanilla
2½ cups powdered sugar, sifted
2 tablespoons chopped walnuts

Heat oven to 350°F with oven rack in middle. Grease and flour a 15 x 10 x 1-inch jellyroll pan.

Mix flour, baking soda, and salt in a medium bowl.

Beat butter and sugar in bowl of a heavy-duty mixer on Medium speed until creamy, scraping down sides of bowl once or twice. Add sour cream, vanilla, and eggs and mix well. Add bananas and beat until mashed. Add flour mixture, and beat on Low just until flour disappears. Stir in walnuts.

Pour batter into prepared pan and spread evenly. Bake 22 to 26 minutes or until a wooden pick inserted in center comes out clean. The cake should spring back when touched lightly with a finger. Cool completely on wire cooling rack before frosting.

FROSTING

Heat brown sugar, butter, and cream in a small saucepan over medium heat, stirring constantly, until it comes to a boil. Continue stirring and boil 30 seconds. Remove from heat and add powdered sugar and vanilla. Beat until smooth.

Spread frosting on bars immediately as frosting sets up quickly. Sprinkle with chopped walnuts. Cut into bars.

SECRETS TO SUCCESS: Sift the powdered sugar for a smooth frosting. Any kind of fine mesh strainer works.

Use some of the finely chopped walnuts that are left over from chopping walnuts for the batter to sprinkle on top. Press lightly into the frosting.

pecan pie bars

If pecan pie is one of your favorites, you'll love these easy-to-make bars. For a fast, fabulous dessert, cut the bars into 2- or 3-inch squares, heat them slightly in the microwave, and top the warm squares with a scoop of vanilla ice cream and a spoonful of caramel sauce.

MAKES 48 BARS

2 cups all-purpose flour
¼ cup firmly packed brown sugar
¾ cup butter, cut-up

FILLING

2¼ cups firmly packed brown sugar
3 eggs, beaten
2 tablespoons butter, melted
1½ teaspoons vanilla
1 cup coarsely chopped pecans, toasted

Heat oven to 350°F with oven rack in middle.

Combine flour and brown sugar in bowl of a heavy-duty mixer. Add butter and beat on Medium speed until mixture resembles coarse crumbs.

Press the crust into bottom and slightly up sides of a 13 x 9-inch baking pan. Bake 12 minutes. The crust will be lightly browned.

FILLING

Beat brown sugar, eggs, butter, and vanilla in same mixer bowl on Low speed until smooth. Stir in pecans. Pour into crust.

Bake 25 to 30 minutes or until set in center. A knife inserted in center will come out clean but wet. Cool on wire cooling rack before cutting. Refrigerate bars.

> BAKER'S NOTE: Toasting the pecans concentrates their flavor. Bake on a small baking pan at 350°F about 6 to 8 minutes. Remove from the pan and cool before using.

chapter five

COOKIES

COOKIES ARE EASY TO BAKE, and that's good news because everyone loves cookies and everyone has a favorite. They are quick to make, using simple techniques, and are easy to take along and share. Baking cookies is a time-honored way to share love between Grandmas, Moms, and children and special friends. Cookies offer a wide variety of flavors, textures, and shapes, depending on their ingredients, mixing technique, and method of baking.

Your basic cookie dough has lots of possibilities. Drop cookies are made from this soft dough, dropped in balls onto a cookie sheet and spread when baked. Shaped cookies are formed into balls or crescents before they are placed on the cookie sheet. Cut-outs come from a firm dough that can be rolled out and cut into myriad shapes before going onto the cookie sheet. Dropped and shaped cookies are easy to make, but cut-outs require a little more practice, just like pie crusts.

As with any baking recipe, it is essential to follow directions carefully and bake at the correct temperature. The size of the cookies, whether they are drop, shaped, or cut-outs, is important because it affects baking times. Use heavy cookie sheets, greased or ungreased, according to the recipe. Because of the high amount of fat in cookies, most bake better on ungreased cookie sheets. A silicone mat really works well for cookies—no sticking and no clean-up. Check the first sheet before the baking time is up to be sure the cookies aren't baking too quickly. Always cool cookie sheets before using a second time, and cool the cookies on wire cooling racks to keep them crisp.

Most cookies are baked from simple doughs consisting of basic ingredients. Because of this simplicity, using only the best ingredients produces the best treats. Use butter or solid vegetable shortening, all-purpose flour, pure vanilla, real chocolate, fresh citrus, and fresh spices. Cookies made with butter tend to be crisp and flat, and cookies with shortening are softer. Many cookie recipes use both fats to produce the best characteristics of each.

The first and most important step to tender cookies is creaming the butter and sugar until light in color, as this incorporates air and adds lightness to the final product. After adding the flour, mix just until it is combined with other ingredients and no longer or gluten will develop and the cookies will not be as tender.

Some doughs need to be chilled before they are baked. This is especially true with cut-out cookie dough. Once the dough is chilled and the butter is firm, it is much easier to roll the dough. Lightly dust the work surface, and cut cookies as close together as possible to avoid re-rolling the dough. Just like biscuits, cookies cut from re-rolled dough will not be as tender. Only work with half of the dough at a time, and chill it if it becomes too soft.

Place cookies on the cookie sheet about 2 inches apart so they have some room to spread. Cut-outs can be placed closer to each other because they don't spread as much. It is best to bake one sheet at a time. If you use two sheets, rotate the sheets inside the oven halfway through baking for even browning. Check the cookies at the minimum baking time, and watch carefully until they are done. Dark cookie sheets bake faster and will brown cookies more readily than shiny cookie sheets. If you like softer cookies, reduce the baking time about 1 minute and remove the cookies when they are still a little moist on top. When cookies are done, they are golden brown on the edges and light brown on top.

While you are learning to bake drop cookies such as the American classic, the chocolate chip cookie, it is a good idea to bake a test cookie from your dough. By just baking one cookie, you will be able to tell if your cookies spread too much. If they do, it's simple to chill the dough briefly and test again. If the dough is still too soft, you can add 1 or 2 tablespoons of flour. The temptation to add flour to a soft dough without testing can produce tough, hard cookies.

Pantry staples are used for cookie baking. I prefer butter, especially for cut-outs, because the cookies have a good buttery flavor and are crisp. Because butter is firm when it is chilled, the dough is easier to roll out. Solid vegetable shortening (such as Crisco) makes cookies that are higher and softer than butter cookies. Softened butter is needed, but if the butter is too soft the cookies will spread too much. Softened butter is butter that has stood at room temperature about 45 minutes. It should still feel firm, but pressing with a finger leaves an imprint. I soften butter in the microwave on defrost. Using defrost is the secret to success. It only takes 30 to 40 seconds but a mistake results in a puddle. Eggs should be at room temperature, but this isn't as important as it is for cakes. All-purpose flour is used most often.

Shiny aluminum cookie sheets are recommended for cookies. Dark cookie sheets brown cookies quickly so the baking time should be watched carefully. Insulated cookie sheets need longer for the cookies to brown, and this tends to make them dry. Cookie cutters come in every size and shape imaginable and for every holiday and season. I use my pizza wheel for cutting and marking dough sometimes. I also find that using a small ice cream scoop to drop dough onto the cookie sheets is really a time-saver.

Crisp cookies can be stored loosely covered at room temperature for several days. Soft cookies are best stored tightly covered. For longer storage of either kind, wrap tightly and freeze. Thaw at room temperature—it only takes a few minutes. When storing cookies, separate crisp and soft cookies and store strong-flavored varieties such as gingerbread cookies in different containers. A piece of parchment or waxed paper placed between the layers prevents cookies from sticking together.

CHOCOLATE CHIP COOKIES DELUXE

· ·

Toll House, or Chocolate Chip, Cookies are definitely the most famous cookies in America. I use both butter and shortening in my recipe—a combination that gives the cookies a buttery flavor and a softer texture. Be creative and experiment with different combinations of "extras," such as butterscotch chips, milk chocolate chunks, and crunchy macadamia nuts.

MAKES 4 DOZEN COOKIES

        2 cups all-purpose flour
        1 teaspoon baking soda
      ½ teaspoon salt
      ½ cup butter, softened
      ½ cup solid vegetable shortening
        1 cup firmly packed brown sugar
      ½ cup granulated sugar
    1 ½ teaspoons vanilla
        1 egg
        1 cup semisweet or milk chocolate chips
        1 cup white chocolate chips
      ½ cup chopped pecans, if desired

Heat oven to 375°F with oven rack in middle (see Baker's Notes below).

Mix flour, baking soda, and salt together in medium bowl.

Beat butter, shortening, brown sugar, and granulated sugar in bowl of a heavy-duty mixer on Medium-High speed until creamy, scraping down bowl once or twice. Add vanilla and egg and mix well.

Reduce mixer speed to Low and add the flour mixture. Scrape down sides of bowl and beat until dough forms. By hand, stir in chocolate chips, white chocolate chips, and pecans.

Drop dough in rounded tablespoons about 2 inches apart onto an ungreased cookie sheet.

Bake 8 to 10 minutes or until cookies are browned on edges. Let cookies stand on cookie sheet for 1 minute before removing them. Cool on wire cooling rack.

These cookies should be stored loosely covered at room temperature.

BAKER'S NOTES: For uniform cookies, I drop the cookie dough onto the cookie sheet using a 1-tablespoon scoop that I purchased at a specialty store.

I usually place my oven racks on the second and fourth levels and bake two cookie sheets at once. If the heat in your oven is uneven, rotate the sheets halfway through baking.

SECRETS TO SUCCESS: Line a cookie sheet with a silicone baking mat or parchment paper for easier clean-up.

If you like softer cookies, remove them from the oven when the edges are barely browned even though the cookies still look slightly moist in the center. They firm up as they cool.

CRISPY OaTmeaL RaISIn COOKIes

Because these cookies contain baking soda instead of baking powder, they will brown better as they are baked and will stay moist longer. This is a very crisp oatmeal cookie, with the chewy raisins providing some softness to an old-fashioned favorite.

MAKES 3 TO 3 ½ DOZEN COOKIES

> 1 ¾ cups all-purpose flour
> 1 teaspoon baking soda
> 1 teaspoon salt
> 1 cup butter, softened
> 1 cup granulated sugar
> 1 cup firmly packed light brown sugar
> 1 teaspoon vanilla
> 2 eggs
> 3 cups quick-cooking oats
> 1 cup raisins or dried cranberries

Heat oven to 350°F with oven rack in middle.

Mix flour, baking soda, and salt in medium bowl.

Beat butter, granulated sugar, and brown sugar in bowl of a heavy-duty mixer on Medium-High speed until creamy, scraping down sides of bowl once or twice. Add vanilla and eggs and mix well.

Reduce mixer speed to Low and add the flour mixture. Scrape down sides of bowl and beat until dough forms. By hand, stir in oats and raisins.

Drop dough in rounded tablespoons about 2 inches apart onto an ungreased cookie sheet.

Bake 8 to 10 minutes or until cookies are browned on edges. Let cookies stand on cookie sheet for 1 minute before removing them. Cool on wire cooling rack.

These cookies should be stored loosely covered at room temperature.

SECRETS TO SUCCESS: Make ice cream sandwiches with vanilla or cinnamon ice cream sandwiched between two cookies. Roll the edges of the sandwich in mini chocolate chips, which will cling to the ice cream. Wrap sandwiches tightly with plastic wrap before freezing. Serve them soon after making so the cookies will still be crisp.

CHOCOLATE MONSTER COOKIES

We call these "dishpan" cookies at my house because if you make the whole recipe, you need a dishpan to mix all the ingredients (or a very large bowl). These cookies traveled with my kids on many team trips and were always "winners." You can use any combination of chocolate chips, butterscotch chips, or M&Ms.

MAKES ABOUT 32 JUMBO COOKIES (or 8 dozen standard cookies)

3 ⅓ cups all-purpose flour
½ cup unsweetened cocoa
2 teaspoons baking powder
2 teaspoons baking soda
1 teaspoon salt
2 cups butter, softened
2 cups granulated sugar
2 cups firmly packed brown sugar
2 teaspoons vanilla
4 eggs

2 cups quick-cooking oats

2 cups cornflakes, lightly crushed

2 cups semisweet chocolate chips, butterscotch chips
or M&Ms (12 ounces)

Heat oven to 350°F with oven rack in middle (see Baker's Notes below). Lightly grease cookie sheets.

Mix flour, cocoa, baking powder, baking soda, and salt together in very large bowl.

Beat butter, granulated sugar, and brown sugar in bowl of a heavy-duty mixer on Medium-High speed until creamy, scraping down sides of bowl once or twice. Add vanilla and eggs and mix well.

Reduce mixer speed to Low and add the flour mixture. Scrape down sides of bowl and beat until dough forms.

Scrape dough back into the very large bowl. Add the oatmeal, corn flakes, and chips and stir until well mixed.

Using a ¼-cup ice cream scoop (or cup measure), drop dough onto cookie sheets. Drop 6 cookies onto each cookie sheet.

Bake 15 to 20 minutes or until set in the center and edges are lightly browned. For softer cookies, reduce baking time slightly. The cookies will still look a little moist in the center. Cool cookies 1 minute on the cookie sheets and then place them on wire cooling racks.

These cookies should be stored loosely covered at room temperature.

BAKER'S NOTES: I usually place my oven racks on the second and fourth levels and bake two cookie sheets at once. If the heat in your oven is uneven, rotate the sheets halfway through baking.

I often make half of the dough into jumbo cookies and the remaining half into smaller cookies. Make smaller cookies by dropping dough, 1 tablespoon at a time, 2 inches apart onto greased cookie sheets. The baking time will be about 10 to 13 minutes.

SECRETS TO SUCCESS: After measuring the cornflakes, I crush them lightly before adding them to the dough so they mix in better.

peanut butter cookies

These cookies are different from other peanut butter cookies because of the contrast between the crunchy salted cocktail peanuts and the sweetness of the cookie. An added benefit is that these cookies are firm and keep well.

MAKES 4 TO 5 DOZEN COOKIES

> 2 ½ cups all-purpose flour
> 1 teaspoon baking powder
> 1 teaspoon baking soda
> ½ teaspoon salt
> 1 cup smooth peanut butter
> ½ cup butter, softened
> ½ cup shortening
> 1 cup granulated sugar
> 1 cup firmly packed brown sugar
> 1 teaspoon vanilla
> 2 eggs
> ¾ cup chopped salted peanuts
> Sugar for rolling

Heat oven to 375°F with oven rack in middle (see Baker's Notes below).

Combine flour, baking powder, baking soda, and salt in medium bowl.

Beat peanut butter, butter, and shortening in bowl of a heavy-duty mixer on Medium-High speed until creamy, scraping down sides of bowl once or twice. Add granulated sugar and brown sugar and beat until mixed. Add vanilla and eggs and mix well.

Reduce mixer speed to Low and add the flour mixture. Scrape down sides of bowl and beat until dough forms. By hand, stir in the peanuts.

Roll about 1 tablespoon of dough into a ball and roll ball in sugar. Try to make the cookies the same size so that baking time will be correct (or adjust baking time). Place dough balls on cookie sheets and press down lightly with a fork, making a crisscross on top.

Bake 10 to 13 minutes until lightly browned. Allow cookies to cool on the cookie sheets 1 minute. Remove and cool completely on wire cooling racks.

BAKER'S NOTES: This recipe can also be used to make chocolate kiss cookies. While the cookies are still warm, press an unwrapped chocolate kiss into each.

Bake two cookie sheets at once. Remember cookies on the lower rack will brown faster on the bottom, and cookies on the upper rack will brown faster on the top. I usually place my oven racks on the second and fourth levels.

SECRETS TO SUCCESS: You can use smooth or crunchy peanut butter.

Dark cookie sheets will bake the cookies more quickly, so check browning before the baking time is up.

I use a 1-tablespoon scoop to drop the dough, but you can also use a measuring spoon.

snickerdoodles

Fragrant cinnamon scents the kitchen when these cookies are in the oven. Due to their unknown origin, possibly from the Pennsylvania Dutch or originally from New England, no one can explain their delightful name. Rolling the dough in cinnamon sugar gives the cookies a crinkly appearance and crunchy sugar coating.

MAKES 4 TO 5 DOZEN

3 cups all-purpose flour
2 teaspoons cream of tartar
1 teaspoon baking soda
½ teaspoon salt
1 cup butter, softened
1 ½ cups sugar
1 teaspoon vanilla
2 eggs

coating

2 tablespoons sugar
2 teaspoons cinnamon

Heat oven to 375°F with oven rack in middle. Lightly grease cookie sheets.

Combine flour, cream of tartar, baking soda and salt in medium bowl.

Beat butter and sugar in bowl of a heavy-duty mixer on Medium-High speed until creamy, scraping down sides of bowl once or twice. Add vanilla and eggs and mix well.

Reduce mixer speed to Low and add the flour mixture. Scrape down sides of bowl and beat until dough forms.

COATING

Mix sugar and cinnamon in shallow dish. I use a custard cup but a saucer also works. Using about 1 tablespoon dough, roll into a ball and roll the ball in the cinnamon sugar. Place on cookie sheets.

Bake 10 to 14 minutes or until lightly browned. Cool on wire cooling racks.

BAKER'S NOTES: Cream of tartar and baking soda are the basic components of baking powder, and they are used here in its place. I think it makes a difference— see if you agree.

I usually place my oven racks on the second and fourth levels and bake two cookie sheets at once. If the heat in your oven is uneven, rotate the sheets halfway through baking.

SECRETS TO SUCCESS: I make enough dough balls to fill a cookie sheet, and then I roll each ball into the cinnamon sugar before baking.

MELTING MOMENTS

These cookies are so delicate and tender, they literally melt in your mouth. The tenderness comes from using cornstarch in place of some of the all-purpose flour. Many cultures have cookies very similar to these, such as Mexican wedding cakes and Russian tea cakes.

MAKES 2½ TO 3 DOZEN COOKIES

> ¾ cup butter, softened
> ½ cup powdered sugar
> 1½ teaspoons vanilla
> 1 cup all-purpose flour
> ½ cup cornstarch
> Powdered sugar for coating

Heat oven to 350°F with oven rack in middle.

Beat butter, powdered sugar, and vanilla in bowl of a heavy-duty mixer on Medium-High speed until creamy, scraping down bowl once or twice.

Reduce mixer speed to Low and add flour and cornstarch. Scrape down sides of bowl and beat until dough forms.

Wrap dough tightly and chill it about 30 minutes if it is too soft to handle.

Roll dough lightly between your palms, using 1 rounded teaspoon of dough, and shape logs about 2½ inches long with tapered ends. Place on an ungreased cookie sheet and curve ends slightly to form crescents. Work quickly so dough doesn't become too soft from the heat of your hands. Chill again if necessary.

Bake 12 to 15 minutes or until golden brown on the edges. Remove from cookie sheet, using a metal spatula. Cool slightly on wire cooling rack.

Roll cookies in powdered sugar while they are still warm and again when cool. Store loosely covered at room temperature.

> BAKER'S NOTE: If the dough becomes too soft to handle, refrigerate it about ½ hour or until firm.
>
> SECRETS TO SUCCESS: I roll the cookies in powdered sugar when they are warm and again when they're cool. If you just roll them once, do it when they are cool.

BASIC BUTTER COOKIES IN FOUR VARIATIONS

Because butter is firm when chilled, I always use it for any cut-out cookie. After chilling dough made with butter, it becomes firm and is easy to roll out. At Christmas my family loves all of the variations below, but at other times I just prepare half of the recipe and cut-out dinosaur cookies for my grandson. He loves to help with the frosting!

MAKES ABOUT 8 DOZEN COOKIES (each fourth of dough makes about 2 dozen)

>
> 5 cups all-purpose flour
> 2 teaspoons baking powder
> ½ teaspoon salt
> 2 cups (1 pound) butter, softened
> 2 cups sugar
> 1 tablespoon vanilla
> 2 eggs
> Decorations: Red- and green-colored sugar, powdered sugar, chocolate decors, ground nuts, food colors

Combine flour, baking powder, and salt in large bowl.

Beat butter and sugar in bowl of a heavy-duty mixer on Medium-High speed until creamy, scraping down sides of bowl once or twice. Add vanilla and eggs and mix well.

Reduce mixer speed to Low, add the flour mixture, and beat until dough forms. At this point, divide the dough into 4 parts. (Chocolate must be added here—see variations below).

Wrap each fourth tightly and refrigerate. Dough keeps several days in the refrigerator. Freeze for longer storage.

CUT-OUT BUTTER COOKIES

ONE-FOURTH OF DOUGH MAKES ABOUT 2 DOZEN COOKIES

Heat oven to 375°F with oven rack in middle. Roll out one part of dough to about ⅛-inch thickness on a lightly floured surface and cut cookies with 3-inch cookie cutters.

If you have any trouble rolling out the cookies, place dough between two sheets of waxed paper or parchment paper before rolling (or chill the dough some more).

Place cookies on an ungreased cookie sheet and decorate as desired. Because of the amount of fat in these cookies, the cookie sheet usually doesn't need to be greased.

Bake 9 to 11 minutes or until edges begin to brown. Cool on wire cooling rack and frost as desired.

FROSTING

2 cups powdered sugar, sifted
¼ cup butter, softened
1 teaspoon vanilla
1½–2 tablespoons whipping cream or milk

Combine powdered sugar, butter, vanilla, and 1 ½ tablespoons cream or milk in mixer bowl of a heavy-duty mixer. Beat on Medium speed until smooth. Add a little more cream if too thick to spread. Divide frosting into small bowls and color as desired. This frosting will frost about 2 dozen cookies.

CHOCOLaTe snOWBaLLS

ONE-FOURTH OF DOUGH MAKES ABOUT 2 DOZEN COOKIES

2 ounces semisweet chocolate, melted

After dough is divided into 4 parts, return one part to mixing bowl. Beat in 2 ounces of melted and cooled semisweet chocolate. Wrap the dough tightly and chill.

Heat oven to 375°F. Shape dough into 1-inch balls and place on cookie sheets, about 2 inches apart. Bake 8 to 10 minutes or until set when touched lightly. Cool on wire cooling rack.

Roll in powdered sugar when warm and again when cool.

SECRETS TO SUCCESS: If you only roll the snowballs in powdered sugar once, do it after the cookies have cooled.

BLACK AND WHITE COOKIES

TWO-FOURTHS OF DOUGH MAKES 4 DOZEN COOKIES

2 ounces semisweet chocolate, melted

After dough is divided into 4 parts, return 1 part to mixing bowl. Beat in 2 ounces of melted and cooled semisweet chocolate.

Roll out the chocolate dough on floured work surface to a 12 x 5-inch rectangle. Roll out the plain dough to another 12 x 5-inch rectangle. Place plain dough on top of chocolate dough. Press layers together and reshape if needed. Cut in half lengthwise and stack dough, forming four layers. If dough is too soft, chill briefly.

Heat oven to 375°F with oven rack in middle. Slice dough into ¼-inch slices and place on cookie sheet. Bake 8 to 10 minutes or until set when touched lightly. Cool on wire cooling rack.

SLICE AND BAKE COOKIES

ONE-FOURTH OF DOUGH MAKES 2 ½ DOZEN COOKIES

Shape one fourth of dough into 2 logs about 1 ¾ inches wide. Roll each log in chocolate decors, finely chopped nuts, or colored sugar. Wrap in plastic wrap and chill until firm.

Heat the oven to 375°F. Slice dough with a sharp knife into ¼-inch slices and place on cookie sheets.

Bake 9 to 11 minutes or until lightly browned. Cool on wire cooling racks.

GInGeR COOKIe SanDWICHeS

The fragrance of these spicy cookies joyfully announces the start of the holiday season! The dough for these cookies is sticky but because it is high in fat, you can add a little flour when working with it. I use unsulfured molasses because I prefer its milder flavor and the spices are highlighted. The cookies taste better the second day because they soften and the flavors blend.

MAKES 18 TO 24 SANDWICH COOKIES

2 ½ cups all-purpose flour
1 teaspoon cinnamon
½ teaspoon baking soda
½ teaspoon ground ginger
¼ teaspoon ground cloves
¼ teaspoon salt
1 cup vegetable shortening
1 cup sugar
⅓ cup mild or strong molasses
1 egg

FILLING

1 container (8 ounces) strawberry cream cheese
¼ cup soft butter
3 cups powdered sugar

Combine flour, cinnamon, baking soda, ginger, cloves, and salt in medium bowl.

Beat shortening and sugar in bowl of a heavy-duty mixer on Medium-High speed until creamy, scraping down sides of bowl once or twice. Add molasses and egg and mix well.

Reduce mixer speed to Low and add the flour mixture. Scrape down sides of bowl and beat until dough forms.

Place 2 large pieces of waxed paper on a work surface. Scrape dough onto waxed paper. Gather dough together with well-floured hands and shape it into a ball. Divide dough in half and wrap well in waxed paper. Refrigerate until firm, about 2 hours. This is a sticky dough until it is chilled.

Heat oven to 375°F with oven rack in middle.

Coat work surface with flour. Roll out dough with a lightly floured rolling pin to ¼-inch thickness. Cut into cookies, using 2½-inch cutters. Place cookies on ungreased cookie sheets.

Bake 10 minutes or until slightly firm to touch and edges begin to brown. Cool on wire cooling rack.

FILLING

For filling, beat cream cheese, butter, and powdered sugar in medium bowl until smooth. Using about 1 tablespoon for each, spread filling on the bottom of half of the cookies; top with the other half placing the bottoms together. Store in the refrigerator.

BAKER'S NOTES: Spices lose flavor over time, so I suggest buying new spices for the best flavor in all your holiday baking.

You can roll the dough out between two sheets of waxed paper. Remove top sheet only to cut-out cookies. Dip cookie cutter into flour occasionally if it is sticking.

SECRET TO SUCCESS: When these cookies are not made into sandwiches, store them loosely covered at room temperature.

ICE BOX COOKIES

Ice Box Cookies are an old-fashioned favorite—the original slice and bake cookies. Their name comes from the fact that the dough was chilled in an ice box, the predecessor of the refrigerator. The cabinet was kept cool with a large block of ice. Brown sugar is the predominant flavor in these crisp cookies that keep well at room temperature.

MAKES 4 TO 5 DOZEN

2 cups all-purpose flour
½ teaspoon cream of tartar
½ teaspoon baking soda
¾ cup butter, softened
1 cup firmly packed brown sugar
1 teaspoon vanilla
1 egg
½ cup chopped pecans

Combine flour, cream of tartar, and baking soda in a medium bowl.

Beat butter and brown sugar in bowl of a heavy-duty mixer on Medium-High speed until creamy, scraping down sides of bowl once or twice. Add vanilla and egg and mix well.

Reduce mixer speed to Low and add the flour mixture. Scrape down sides of bowl and beat until dough forms. Add pecans.

Divide dough into 3 parts. Shape each part into a roll about 2 inches in diameter. Wrap each roll tightly in waxed paper or plastic wrap and chill about 2 hours or until firm.

Heat oven to 375°F with oven rack in middle.

Unwrap dough and cut into slices about ¼ inch thick. Place cookies on ungreased cookie sheets, about 2 inches apart.

Bake 8 to 10 minutes or until edges become lightly browned. Cool on wire cooling racks.

> BAKER'S NOTES: Use a serrated knife or a very sharp knife to slice the cookies, and rotate the dough after each cut to maintain their round shape.
>
> I usually place my oven racks on the second and fourth levels and bake two cookie sheets at once. If the heat in your oven is uneven, rotate the sheets halfway through baking.
>
> SECRETS TO SUCCESS: I store some of this dough in the freezer for baking cookies at the last minute.

nuT KoLaches

The ground pecan filling in this cookie is similar to that in rugulach, a well-known Jewish pastry with European origins. Kolaches have the flavor of an old-fashioned nut roll but are much easier to make. Because they freeze well, you can make them ahead and freeze them until needed. Use a food processor to grind the nuts.

MAKES 2 ½ DOZEN COOKIES

½ cup milk
1 (¼-ounce) package active dry yeast
1 teaspoon vanilla
1 egg, beaten
3 cups all-purpose flour
¼ cup sugar
½ teaspoon salt
1 cup cold butter, cut into ½-inch pieces

FILLING

>2 egg whites
>6 tablespoons sugar
>1 cup ground pecans or walnuts
>2 tablespoons butter, melted
>>Powdered sugar

Heat oven to 350°F with oven rack in middle.

Warm milk in small saucepan until it is warm to the touch (105 to 115°F). Sprinkle yeast over the milk and let stand 5 minutes. Stir in vanilla and egg.

Place flour, sugar, salt, and butter in bowl of a heavy-duty mixer. Beat on Low speed until mixture resembles coarse crumbs with some pea-sized pieces.

Beat in the milk mixture, scraping down sides of bowl once or twice. When soft dough forms, gather dough together, divide in half, and wrap tightly in plastic wrap. Chill dough while you make the filling.

FILLING

Beat egg whites in bowl of a heavy-duty mixer on high speed until soft peaks form. Gradually beat in sugar and continue beating until stiff peaks form. Fold in pecans and melted butter.

Lightly grease cookie sheets. Place half of the dough on a lightly floured work surface. Dust the rolling pin with a little flour. Roll out dough to ¼ inch thickness. Cut dough into 3-inch squares. Place 1 teaspoon filling in center of each square. Fold two opposite corners to the center, overlapping slightly. Press down the folded corners. Place on cookie sheets. Repeat with the remaining dough.

Bake 10 to 14 minutes or until lightly browned. Cool on wire cooling racks. Sprinkle with powdered sugar.

> BAKER'S NOTE: It is tempting to place a little more filling on each cookie, but it will only ooze out during baking.

PISTACHIO BISCOTTI

With a gourmet coffee bar on every corner, biscotti have become familiar to everyone. Biscotti are actually Italian twice-baked cookies, perfect for dipping into hot espresso. These biscotti are slightly moist, not as hard as some others.

MAKES 2 ½ TO 3 DOZEN BISCOTTI

>   2 cups all-purpose flour
>   1 teaspoon baking powder
>   ¼ teaspoon salt
>   ¼ cup butter, softened
>   ¾ cup firmly packed brown sugar
>   1 teaspoon vanilla
>   2 eggs, beaten
>   ½ cup chopped pistachio nuts (about 4 ounces unshelled)
>   ½ cup white chocolate chips

Heat oven to 350°F with oven rack in middle. Line a cookie sheet with parchment paper or lightly grease.

Combine flour, baking powder, and salt in medium bowl.

Beat butter and brown sugar in bowl of a heavy-duty mixer on Medium-High speed until creamy, scraping down sides of bowl once or twice. Add vanilla and eggs, one at a time, beating after each, and scrape down sides of bowl once or twice.

Reduce mixer speed to Low speed and add the flour mixture. Scrape down sides of bowl and beat until dough forms. By hand, stir in pistachios and white chocolate chips.

Gather dough together on lightly floured work surface and divide in half. If dough is slightly sticky, dust your hands with flour. Shape each half into a 12-inch log and place on prepared cookie sheet, about 4 inches apart. Flatten logs slightly.

Bake 18 to 20 minutes or until firm to the touch. Reduce oven temperature to 300°F. Allow logs to cool 15 minutes. Slice logs diagonally into ¾-inch slices. Return slices to the cookie sheet.

Bake 8 to 12 minutes longer or until lightly browned, turning slices over once to toast second side. Cool on wire cooling rack. Store tightly covered.

BAKER'S NOTE: I find it easiest to cut the logs on a cutting board, using a serrated knife. Use a long spatula to remove the logs to the board. You can cut the logs in half if necessary to move them.

SECRETS TO SUCCESS: Buy unshelled pistachio nuts that have not been dyed red. The shells should be slightly opened, which is a sign of mature nuts and makes them easier to shell.

chapter six

CRISPS and COBBLERS

DO YOU REMEMBER picking apples on a brilliant fall day and the fragrance that filled the house as they were baked into a cinnamon-scented apple crisp? Baking a crisp or a cobbler, bubbling with slightly thickened juices and covered with a sweet crumbly topping, is one of the best ways to enjoy the freshest fruits in any season. A homemade dessert makes any meal special, and these fruit desserts that sparkle with sweet and tangy flavors have been popular since colonial times.

Crisps, Cobblers, and Brown Bettys are part of a group of dishes known as American Fruit Desserts that evolved from Old World recipes as country bakers used whatever fruit was in season and added an uncomplicated topping.

The definitions of these desserts vary, but for me, a crisp has a sweet, crunchy topping, usually with oats providing the crunch; a cobbler has tender biscuit dough baked over juicy fruit. Brown Bettys are the simplest of all. Juicy fruit is sweetened and layered with buttery breadcrumbs before baking.

After you learn how to put together a spicy streusel topping with lots of cinnamon, sprinkle it over fresh fruit and bake. Make crisps with apples, pears, plums, peaches, or any combination of fruits in season. A little lemon juice often is added to prevent apples or pears from turning brown and to balance the sweetness.

A cobbler topping is prepared like biscuit dough but contains more liquid, making the dough softer. In a cobbler, the soft dough dropped onto hot and bubbly fruit bakes to a tender and flaky topping. Cobblers often are made with freshly picked berries but peach cobbler is one of my favorites.

Supermarkets often have information on locally grown fruit, especially apples, to help you select a local variety. To purchase oats for a crisp topping, look for boxes of "oats"—oatmeal actually is cooked oats. Choose old-fashioned or quick-cooking oats, depending on the recipe.

Most crisp toppings require cutting in butter with a pastry blender until the mixture resembles coarse crumbs with some pea-sized pieces. The same method is used to cut in the butter or shortening when making the biscuit dough for cobblers. The biscuit topping on cobblers needs to be baked until golden brown. Bake crisps, cobblers, and brown Bettys until crisp fruits are fork-tender and the slightly thickened juices are bubbling away.

Serve these homespun desserts warm with ice cream, whipped cream, or crème fraiche. Fruit desserts can be made ahead and reheated in the oven to maintain their characteristic crispness. They are best eaten the day they are made, but any remaining dessert should be refrigerated.

Colonial kitchens had many limits, including equipment, so very little is needed for preparing American Fruit Desserts. All you need is a sharp knife and a heatproof deep baking dish. A vegetable peeler makes it easy to peel fruit but isn't essential. I recommend having deep-dish pie plates, a 1½- or 2-quart casserole, and an 8- or 9-inch square baking dish. The basic requirement for the baking dish is that it is large enough to hold the fruit and topping without fruit juice bubbling over into the oven. A pastry blender makes it easier to cut in the butter for a streusel topping but is not essential.

caramel apple CRISP

A crisp, the simplest of American Fruit Desserts, requires little but seasonal fruit and an old-fashioned crisp topping. Here, tart apples bake under a rich caramel sauce. I have baked this comforting fall dessert with many varieties of apples. Experiment with local apples and decide which you like best.

MAKES 8 SERVINGS

6 cups peeled sliced apples (6 to 8 medium)
½ cup firmly packed dark or light brown sugar
¼ cup all-purpose flour
¼ teaspoon freshly grated nutmeg or pinch of ground nutmeg
1 tablespoon lemon juice
½ cup caramel sauce

TOPPING

½ cup old-fashioned oats
½ cup all-purpose flour
½ cup firmly packed light brown sugar
¼ cup cold butter, cut-up
Vanilla ice cream, if desired

Heat oven to 375°F with oven rack in middle.

Combine apples, dark brown sugar, flour, nutmeg, and lemon juice in large bowl. Stir until fruit is well coated.

Spoon apple mixture into 2-quart casserole or 11 x 7-inch baking dish. Heat caramel sauce slightly and drizzle it over the fruit.

TOPPING

Combine oats, flour, and light brown sugar in medium bowl. Cut in butter with a pastry blender until mixture resembles coarse crumbs with some pea-sized pieces. Crumble over the fruit.

Bake 55 to 60 minutes or until bubbling all over and apples are fork-tender. Cool slightly and serve with ice cream.

> BAKER'S NOTES: Use an apple variety recommended for cooking, such as Gala, Golden Delicious, Rome Beauty, or Granny Smith.
>
> Use either old-fashioned or quick-cooking oats in this recipe.
>
> SECRETS TO SUCCESS: The flavor of freshly grated nutmeg is not as sharp as ground, so only use a pinch of ground nutmeg.

BLUEBERRY RHUBARB CRUMBLE

Fresh, sweet blueberries tame the tartness of rhubarb in this British crumble. Rhubarb is traditionally a sign of spring, and I always buy extra when I go to the farmers' market or find it at the supermarket. It can be frozen without washing or trimming but should be tightly wrapped.

MAKES 8 SERVINGS

1 ½ cups sugar
¾ cup all-purpose flour, divided
1 teaspoon cinnamon
6 cups chopped fresh rhubarb
1 ½ cups fresh blueberries
¼ cup orange juice, or water

TOPPING

> ½ cup firmly packed brown sugar
> ¼ cup cold butter, cut-up

Heat oven to 350°F with oven rack in center. Spray bottom of a 9 x 9-inch baking dish or 1½-quart casserole with nonstick cooking spray.

Mix granulated sugar with ¼ cup of flour and cinnamon in large bowl. Add rhubarb, blueberries, and orange juice and stir until fruit is well coated. Be careful not to break the blueberries. Spoon into prepared baking dish.

Bake 30 minutes or until juices are starting to thicken and bubble.

TOPPING

Mix remaining ½ cup of flour with the brown sugar. Cut in butter with a pastry blender until mixture resembles coarse crumbs with some pea-sized pieces. Crumble over the hot fruit.

Bake 25 to 35 minutes longer or until juices are bubbling and rhubarb is fork-tender. Cool on wire cooling rack.

Serve warm or at room temperature. Store any remaining in refrigerator.

BAKER'S NOTE: Because frozen rhubarb and frozen blueberries are available through-out the year, this dessert can be baked any time. When you are using frozen rhubarb, I suggest chopping the largest pieces. Use the rhubarb and blueberries while still frozen. After adding the topping, you will need to bake about 60 minutes longer.

SECRETS TO SUCCESS: When I serve this dessert warm, I offer it with a little cream.

CRISPY OaTMeaL PLUM CRUNCH

Summer and early fall are the best time to find plums in the supermarket or at the farmers' market. I like that special spark of tartness from the skin, followed with the sweet, juicy taste of the fruit. Plums are becoming more readily available year round due to imports from South America. I like to serve this dessert with crème fraiche.

MAKES 8 SERVINGS

½ cup sugar
2 tablespoons all-purpose flour
1 teaspoon cinnamon
1 teaspoon grated lemon peel
6 cups sliced plums (about 2 pounds)
1 tablespoon lemon juice

TOPPING

½ cup all- purpose flour
½ cup quick-cooking oats
⅓ cup firmly packed brown sugar
¼ cup cold butter, cut-up

Heat oven to 375°F with oven rack in middle. Spray bottom of 11 x 7-inch baking dish or 2-quart casserole with nonstick cooking spray.

Mix granulated sugar, 2 tablespoons flour, cinnamon, and lemon peel in large bowl. Add plums and lemon juice and stir until fruit is well coated. Spoon fruit into baking dish.

TOPPING

Mix flour, oats, and brown sugar in small bowl. Cut in butter with a pastry blender until mixture resembles coarse crumbs with some pea-sized pieces. Crumble over the fruit.

Bake 35 to 45 minutes or until juices are bubbling all over and topping is golden brown. Cool slightly before serving—the sweet fruit syrup makes it very hot. Serve warm or at room temperature. Store any remaining in refrigerator.

> BAKER'S NOTE: Ripe plums yield to a little pressure around the stem end. I often ripen plums at room temperature for a few days after I purchase them.
>
> SECRETS TO SUCCESS: Grate the lemon peel before cutting the lemon and squeezing it for juice.

autumn apple crisp

On a cool, rainy day, brighten your kitchen with the sweet aroma of baking apples. Sweet, pure maple syrup balances the welcome tartness of the Granny Smith apples. Spoon some of the juices over the fruit when you serve this. Sometimes I add a spoonful of Custard Sauce (see page 284) to dress it up.

MAKES 4 TO 6 SERVINGS

½ cup firmly packed brown sugar
2 tablespoons all-purpose flour
4 cups peeled sliced apples (4 to 6 medium)
⅓ cup maple syrup

TOPPING

⅓ cup all-purpose flour
⅓ cup quick-cooking oats
⅓ cup firmly packed brown sugar
½ teaspoon cinnamon
¼ cup cold butter, cut-up
¼ cup chopped walnuts

Heat oven to 375°F with oven rack in middle.

Mix brown sugar with 2 tablespoons flour in medium bowl and add apples. Toss until apples are well coated. Pour maple syrup over apples and stir to mix. Spoon fruit into 9-inch pie plate or 8 x 8-inch baking dish.

TOPPING

Mix flour, oats, brown sugar, and cinnamon in medium bowl. Cut in butter with a pastry blender until mixture resembles coarse crumbs with some pea-sized pieces. Stir in walnuts. Crumble topping over the apples.

Bake 30 to 35 minutes or until topping is browned and crispy and apples are fork-tender. Serve warm or at room temperature. (I think it tastes best warm from the oven.)

BAKER'S NOTE: Pure maple syrup adds the best flavor here, but pancake syrup can be used in its place. Some supermarkets have Grade B maple syrup, which is less expensive than Grade A.

CRANBERRY PEAR CRISP

Pears usually need a few days to ripen at room temperature. To determine if they are ripe, press gently at the stem end. The fruit should give a little, but the sides of the pears will still feel fairly firm. The pears will soften when they are baked. I often mix pears and apples to make the 8 cups of fruit needed here.

MAKES 12 SERVINGS

¾ cup sugar
2 tablespoons all-purpose flour
1 tablespoon lemon juice
8 cups peeled sliced pears (8 pears)
1 (10-ounce) container frozen cranberry-orange sauce

TOPPING

½ cup quick-cooking oats
⅓ cup all-purpose flour
⅓ cup firmly packed brown sugar
¼ cup cold butter, cut-up
½ cup sliced almonds

Heat oven to 375°F with oven rack in middle. Lightly spray 13 x 9-inch baking dish with nonstick cooking spray.

Combine sugar, flour, and lemon juice in large bowl. Gently stir in pears and cranberry-orange sauce and spoon mixture into baking dish.

TOPPING

Mix oats, flour, and brown sugar in medium bowl. Cut in butter with a pastry blender until mixture resembles coarse crumbs with some pea-sized pieces. Stir in almonds. Crumble topping over the pears.

Bake 45 to 55 minutes or until topping is browned and crispy and pears are fork-tender. Serve warm.

> BAKER'S NOTE: The cranberry-orange sauce doesn't need to be thawed. It's soft enough to use when frozen.
>
> SECRETS TO SUCCESS: Toss in ½ cup of dried cranberries for a tangy accent and omit the frozen cranberry-orange sauce.

aPPLe anD PeaR BROWn BeTTy

Brown Betty is a traditional American dessert made with breadcrumbs and fruit. During baking, the fruit juices and buttery crumbs combine to make a rich syrup. I use Granny Smith apples and D'Anjou pears because I like the contrast between the tart apple and the sweet pear.

MAKES 8 TO 10 SERVINGS

> 2 cups soft breadcrumbs
> ¼ cup butter, melted
> 4 cups peeled sliced apples (about 4 medium)
> 4 cups peeled sliced pears (about 4 medium)
> ½ cup firmly packed brown sugar
> 1 teaspoon grated orange peel
> 2 tablespoons freshly squeezed orange juice

Heat oven to 375°F with oven rack in middle.

Combine breadcrumbs and butter in small bowl and stir with a fork until crumbs are evenly coated.

Toss apples and pears with brown sugar, orange peel, and orange juice in large bowl. Spoon about half of the fruit into a 2-quart casserole or 8 x 8-inch baking dish. Top with half the breadcrumbs. Repeat with the remaining fruit and breadcrumbs.

Bake 45 to 55 minutes or until crumbs are browned and fruits are fork-tender. Cool slightly before serving.

> BAKER'S NOTE: I use an 8-ounce loaf of firm bread, such as French bread with the crust cut off, to make soft breadcrumbs in the food processor or blender.

TROPICAL FRUIT COBBLER

A blustery winter's day is the ideal time to taste tropical fruits and dream of warm Caribbean breezes. By adding the coconut and macadamia nuts at the end, they are lightly toasted. A sherbet or fruity sorbet is the perfect accompaniment.

MAKES 8 TO 10 SERVINGS

4 cups cubed pineapple (1 pineapple)
2 cups sliced mango
2 bananas, peeled and sliced into 1- to 2-inch pieces
2 tablespoons lemon juice
½ cup firmly packed brown sugar
2 tablespoons all-purpose flour
1 teaspoon grated lime peel

TOPPING
1½ cups all-purpose flour
⅓ cup firmly packed brown sugar
1 teaspoon baking powder

¼ teaspoon salt

⅓ cup cold butter, cut-up

½ cup milk

 1 egg, beaten

⅓ cup chopped macadamia nuts

¼ cup flaked sweetened coconut

      Lime or orange sherbet, if desired

Heat oven to 400°F with oven rack in middle.

Toss pineapple, mango, and bananas with lemon juice in large bowl.

Combine brown sugar, flour, and lime in small bowl. Add to fruit mixture and toss gently.

Spoon mixture into 2-quart casserole or 11 x 7-inch baking dish. Bake 20 to 30 minutes or until juices are bubbling.

TOPPING

Mix flour, brown sugar, baking powder, and salt together in medium bowl. Cut in butter with a pastry blender until topping resembles coarse crumbs with some pea-sized pieces.

Combine milk and egg in small bowl. Add to the flour mixture and stir just until a soft sticky dough forms. Drop dough over the hot fruit along the edges of the dish, leaving the center open.

Bake 15 minutes longer until topping is beginning to brown. Sprinkle with the macadamias and coconut, and bake 5 to 10 minutes more until juices are bubbling in center and coconut is toasted.

BAKER'S NOTE: Chilled fresh sliced pineapple and mango are found throughout the year in the produce section of most supermarkets.

If you purchase fresh mangoes, look for rosy red fruit that yield slightly to pressure.

SECRETS TO SUCCESS: To cook the biscuit topping completely, it needs to be placed over hot, bubbling fruit. Otherwise the biscuits will be doughy on the bottom.

GINGERBREAD
nectarine cobbler

During the Middle Ages, ginger and pepper were the only spices available to bakers, which explains the historical popularity of gingerbread. Gingerbread and gingerbread men are a holiday tradition for many nationalities. In the winter, sometimes I bake this with thawed frozen peach slices and frozen blueberries.

MAKES 8 TO 10 SERVINGS

½ cup firmly packed brown sugar
¼ cup all-purpose flour
4 cups peeled sliced nectarines (4 to 6 nectarines)
2 cups mixed berries
1 tablespoon lemon juice
1 teaspoon grated lemon peel

GINGERBREAD

1 cup all-purpose flour
½ teaspoon baking powder
½ teaspoon baking soda
½ teaspoon cinnamon
½ teaspoon ground ginger
¼ teaspoon ground nutmeg
¼ teaspoon salt
½ cup firmly packed brown sugar
⅓ cup vegetable shortening
⅓ cup mild or strong molasses
1 egg
⅓ cup lowfat buttermilk

Heat oven to 350°F with oven rack in middle. Lightly grease 11 x 7-inch baking dish.

Combine brown sugar and flour in large bowl. Stir in fruit, lemon juice, and lemon peel. Toss gently to coat fruit. Spoon fruit into prepared baking dish.

Bake 20 minutes or until fruit juices are starting to bubble.

GINGERBREAD

Sift flour, baking powder, baking soda, cinnamon, ginger, nutmeg, and salt together into medium bowl.

Beat brown sugar and shortening in bowl of a heavy-duty mixer on Medium speed until light and fluffy. Beat in molasses and egg. Scrape down sides of bowl.

Reduce mixer speed to Low. Add half of the flour mixture and mix. Beat in all of the buttermilk and scrape down sides of bowl. Add remaining flour mixture and beat until smooth. Drop mounds of batter onto the hot fruit.

Bake 40 to 50 minutes longer or until gingerbread springs back when touched lightly. You can test with a toothpick, but only insert it into the gingerbread. Cool slightly and serve warm with whipped cream.

BAKER'S NOTES: Unsulphured molasses has a milder flavor and lighter color that sulphured molasses. Look on the bottle to see how the molasses has been processed.

Because the skin on nectarines is tender, they don't have to be peeled.

SECRETS TO SUCCESS: Sifting assures that the spices are evenly distributed. If you don't have a sifter, use a wire mesh strainer.

---

summer fruit cobbler

· ·

Bite into a ripe, juicy peach or nectarine and you've captured the essence of summer. For this recipe, I buy whatever fruit looks best at the market and often use several kinds. Fruits can be ripened at room temperature by placing them in a paper bag for a day or so.

MAKES 6 TO 8 SERVINGS

¼ cup sugar
2 tablespoons all-purpose flour
2 cups sliced fresh peaches (about 3 medium)
2 plums, sliced
1 cup blueberries
2 tablespoons Amaretto liqueur or 1 teaspoon almond extract
1 tablespoon lemon juice

TOPPING

1 cup all-purpose flour
¼ cup sugar
1 teaspoon baking powder
¼ teaspoon salt
½ cup whipping cream
1 egg, beaten
3 tablespoons slivered almonds

Heat oven to 375°F with oven rack in middle.

Mix sugar and 2 tablespoons flour in large bowl. Add fruit and toss gently to coat. Add Amaretto and lemon juice. Spoon mixture into a 9 x 9-inch baking dish or 1½-quart casserole.

TOPPING

Mix flour, sugar, baking powder, and salt together in medium bowl.

Beat whipping cream and egg in small bowl. Add mixture to the flour mixture and stir until a soft, sticky dough forms.

Drop dough over the fruit along edges of pan, leaving the center open. Sprinkle almonds over the dough.

Bake 35 to 40 minutes or until topping is golden brown and juices are bubbling. Serve warm with ice cream. Store any remaining in refrigerator.

BAKER'S NOTES: To peel the peaches, drop them into boiling water for 20 seconds. Remove and place them in cold water. The skins will slip off easily, and you can then slice the fruit.

Because the fruit will not be completely covered by the topping, it will be easier to determine when the topping is baked.

SECRETS TO SUCCESS: For the lightest topping, the dough should be a little stickier that biscuit dough.

savory chicken cobbler

"Cobbler" refers to something actually "cobbled" together from what's available, and this concept as it relates to baking dates back to colonial times. Here a homey biscuit topping bakes over hot chicken and vegetables for a one-dish meal.

MAKES 4 TO 6 SERVINGS

1 tablespoon olive oil
1 cup thinly sliced leek (1 leek), or chopped onion
1 (8-ounce) package sliced mushrooms
3 tablespoons all-purpose flour
1½ cups chicken broth
2 cups cubed cooked chicken
2 cups frozen mixed vegetables
½ teaspoon salt
Pepper, to taste

BISCUIT TOPPING

1 cup all-purpose flour
1½ teaspoons baking powder
1 teaspoon chopped fresh thyme or pinch of dried thyme
¼ teaspoon salt
¼ cup solid vegetable shortening
⅓ cup milk

Heat oven to 400°F with oven rack in middle.

Heat oil in 9-inch skillet and cook leek over medium heat, stirring occasionally, until it is transparent and tender. Add mushrooms and cook over Medium-High heat until they soften, stirring often.

Sprinkle flour over vegetables and mix well. Stir in chicken broth and continue stirring until sauce thickens. Add chicken, mixed vegetables, and salt. Season to taste with pepper. Bring sauce to a boil. Pour mixture into 2-quart casserole or 11 x 7-inch baking dish.

BISCUIT TOPPING

Mix flour, baking powder, thyme, and salt in medium bowl. Cut in shortening with a pastry blender until mixture resembles coarse crumbs with some pea-sized pieces. Add milk and stir until a soft, sticky dough forms. Drop dough onto hot chicken mixture, forming 4 to 6 biscuits.

Bake 23 to 27 minutes or until biscuit topping is browned and cooked through.

BAKER'S NOTES: Leeks have a subtle and delicate onion flavor. To use the leek, cut off the root end and trim the white stalk to about 2 inches above the green. Slice the stalk into quarters from top to bottom and rinse until all the dirt in removed. Pat dry with paper towels and cut into thin slices.

The frozen mixed vegetables do not need to be thawed.

SECRETS TO SUCCESS: For cooked chicken, you can save time by using a rotisserie chicken from the supermarket.

You can prepare the chicken and vegetables ahead and refrigerate. Heat the chicken mixture, cover with the biscuit topping, and bake just before serving.

chapter seven

. . . .

CUSTARDS anD
BREaD PUDDINGS

BAKED CUSTARDS AND BREAD PUDDINGS are sweet and savory custard dishes thickened with eggs. Breakfast casseroles, called stratas, are actually savory bread puddings, puffed and airy from many kinds of bread and flavored with cheeses and various fillings.

Baked custard is the simplest of all egg dishes—all you need is milk, sugar, and eggs. As these desserts bake, the eggs thicken the milk, forming a creamy pudding. Milk is the liquid used most often for baked custard, but for a richer, silkier texture, you can replace the milk with whipping cream or half-and-half without changing the recipe. Baked custards have been "comfort foods" for many generations because they are easily digested and nourishing.

Baking any custard in a water bath provides a gentle, even heat and prevents the eggs from overcooking on the edges before the centers are set. Overcooking egg custards results in "weeping," a term for the liquid being squeezed out by the egg proteins, causing them to curdle and become watery. Any custard that doesn't contain a starch, such as flour, cornstarch or bread should be baked in a water bath.

A heatproof container that is at least 2 inches larger than the baking dish or custard cups is needed for a water bath. Most bread puddings and stratas don't require a water bath because the addition of bread and other ingredients protects the eggs from overcooking. Six custard cups will fit into a 13 x 9-inch baking pan. Partially slide out the oven rack, place the larger pan for the water bath on it, and add the custard cups. Using a glass measuring cup with a spout, pour very hot tap water into the outer container. It is important to prevent any water from spilling into the custard. You will need about ½ inch of hot water surrounding the custards.

Carefully push the rack into the oven and bake. Be very careful with this process, as it is easy to get burned with a wet potholder.

Once you learn to test for doneness, you'll know the secret of how easy these dishes are to prepare. Baked custards and puddings are done baking when a knife inserted near the center comes out clean. The knife will be wet but shouldn't have any egg clinging to it. Because the custards continue to bake after they are removed from the oven, they should be removed—outer pan and all—when they are still slightly soft in the center. Remove them from the water bath for the same reason and cool on a wire rack.

Custard cups or ramekins are used for individual custards. Crème brulée, the superstar of this category, is baked in crème brulée dishes that are very shallow. A kitchen torch for caramelizing the sugar on a crème brulée is fun to have, but placing the dishes under the broiler can also create the crunchy topping. Some custards are baked in deep-dish pie plates, and many bread puddings are baked in heatproof 13 x 9-inch dishes or casseroles. Use a whisk to thoroughly mix the liquids and a strainer to remove bits of egg that won't dissolve in baking—the same strainer that you use for sifting flour.

CLASSIC CRÈME CARAMEL

Is there anything more comforting than the luscious creaminess of baked custard? Although custard consists only of eggs, milk, sugar, and usually vanilla, after gently baking, it is transformed into the original comfort food. After the custard has been baked and chilled, the caramelized sugar dissolves and bathes the custard in a sweet sauce. You can also serve custards with some fresh berries or a dollop of whipped cream.

MAKES 6 SERVINGS

> 1 cup sugar, divided
> 3 tablespoons water
> 2 drops lemon juice
> 3 eggs, beaten
> ⅛ teaspoon salt
> 1 teaspoon vanilla
> 2½ cups warm whole milk

Heat oven to 350°F with oven rack in middle. Lightly butter six 6-ounce custard cups or ramekins and place in a 13 x 9-inch baking pan.

Cook ½ cup sugar, water and lemon juice in heavy medium saucepan over medium-high heat until sugar dissolves. Swirl pan, rinsing any sugar off its sides. Reduce heat to medium and cook until the syrup turns a deep golden color, about 3 to 4 minutes.

Immediately pour a little caramel into each custard cup—you will only get one chance because it hardens instantly. It is very hot, so be careful and use potholders.

Beat eggs, remaining ½ cup sugar, salt, and vanilla in large bowl until blended. Slowly beat in warm milk. Strain milk mixture through a mesh strainer and pour about ½ cup into each custard cup.

Place pan with custard cups on the oven rack and pour hot water into pan to a depth of about ½ inch.

Bake 35 to 40 minutes or until the custards are almost set and a knife inserted near the center comes out clean although it will be wet.

Cool to room temperature, cover and refrigerate at least 4 hours. Chill overnight to allow the caramel to liquefy.

To unmold the custards, run a metal spatula around the sides of each cup. Cover cup with a serving plate and invert. The custard will slide out. Store custards in the refrigerator.

BAKER'S NOTE: Test for doneness about ½ inch away from the center as the custards will finish baking after they are removed from the oven. Be careful not to get water on your potholder or you can get burned.

The caramel is my favorite part, but you can prepare the custard without it. You really don't have to chill the cups before serving, but it is necessary if you want to unmold the custard and allow the caramel syrup to dissolve. I usually can't wait that long!

SECRET TO SUCCESS: I always use whole milk for custard because it makes the custard creamier, but you can use fat-free, 1%, or 2% milk.

CHAI LATTE EGG CUSTARD

Chai latte is a popular beverage made with black or green tea and milk and flavored with aromatic spices such as cinnamon and cloves. It is usually sweetened and served hot and adds just a hint of spice in this dessert. Serve custards with a little whipped cream and sprinkle with cinnamon.

MAKES 6 SERVINGS

⅓ cup sugar
2 eggs
2 egg yolks
Pinch of salt
1 teaspoon vanilla
1½ cups warm half-and-half
1 cup liquid chai concentrate
Freshly grated nutmeg

Heat oven to 350°F with oven rack in middle. Place six 6-ounce custard cups in 13 x 9-inch baking pan.

Beat sugar, eggs, egg yolks, salt, and vanilla in large bowl until blended. Slowly beat in warm half-and-half and chai concentrate. Strain milk mixture through a mesh strainer and pour about ½ cup into each custard cup.

Place baking pan with custard cups on rack in oven and pour hot water into pan to a depth of about ½ inch.

Use fresh nutmeg, and grate a little over each cup, or add just a pinch of ground nutmeg.

Bake 35 to 40 minutes or until custards are almost set in the center and a knife inserted near center comes out clean although it will be wet.

Be careful to keep your potholder dry when removing the pan from the oven. Remove custards from the hot water and cool.

After custards are cooled, they should be refrigerated. They can be served warm or chilled. I serve these custards with a little whipped cream.

BAKER'S NOTE: Strain the milk mixture into a large glass measuring cup and it will be easy to pour into the custard cups.

SECRETS TO SUCCESS: Whole nutmeg looks like an acorn and is available at most supermarkets and specialty stores. It is easy to grate over the custards, using a microplane or other grater. Ground nutmeg has a stronger flavor than fresh and should be used sparingly.

I have found it easy to use liquid chai concentrate, but other kinds of chai can be used. For the best flavor in these custards, do not prepare chai with the full amount of water specified on the package

NEW ORLEANS BREAD PUDDING WITH BANANAS FOSTER SAUCE

Day-old French bread is the traditional type of bread used for this pudding, but I have also used cinnamon swirl bread and croissants for a richer dessert. The banana sauce is a classic from New Orleans, created at Brennan's restaurant and usually served over ice cream.

MAKES 9 SERVINGS

6 cups 1-inch pieces of day-old French bread
¾ cup sugar
1 teaspoon vanilla
3 eggs
2 cups milk
Freshly grated nutmeg, if desired

sauce

¼ cup butter
½ cup firmly packed brown sugar
1 tablespoon lemon juice
2 tablespoons crème de banana liqueur, if desired
3 bananas, peeled and sliced
¼ cup warm dark rum

Heat oven to 350°F with oven rack in middle. Lightly spray 9 x 9-inch baking dish with nonstick cooking spray. Place bread in baking dish.

Beat sugar, vanilla, and eggs in large bowl until blended. Slowly beat in milk. Strain milk mixture through a mesh strainer, and pour over the bread.

Let dish stand at room temperature about 30 minutes or until bread has absorbed the milk mixture. Press any bread that is not moist into the liquid.

Bake 45 to 55 minutes or until set in the center and a knife inserted near center comes out clean although it will be wet.

Cool slightly before serving warm with the sauce, or cool to room temperature and refrigerate.

sauce

Melt butter in 9-inch skillet. Add brown sugar and lemon juice and cook over medium heat, stirring constantly, until a sauce forms. Stir in crème de banana. Add banana slices and heat until warm. Ignite the warm rum and pour into the sauce.

Cut pudding into squares and place in individual serving dishes.

Spoon the hot sauce over the pudding.

BAKER'S NOTE: I think the flavor of freshly grated nutmeg is not as sharp as ground nutmeg, and I like it sprinkled lightly on this dessert.

SECRETS TO SUCCESS: Because dark rum is aged longer than light or medium rum, it has a smoother flavor that enhances desserts. Myers' rum is the well-known dark Jamaican rum that I use.

The rum must be warm to ignite. Warm it in a small saucepan and ignite it using a gas lighter or a long match because the flames flare up. I have also heated the rum in a metal ladle, ignited it, and poured it into the sauce.

Only try to ignite the rum once. If you keep adding more rum, the pudding will be overwhelmed with it.

WILD MUSHROOM BREAD PUDDING

I like to serve savory this side dish with juicy slices of roast beef or tender steaks. Shiitake mushrooms should be plump with edges that turn under and not dried out. Remove the tough stems before cooking. Dried porcini mushrooms need to be rehydrated in hot water.

MAKES 9 SERVINGS

2 ½ cups milk

2 eggs, beaten

½ teaspoon salt

3 cups day-old bread cubes

2 cups herb seasoned shredded stuffing

2 tablespoons olive oil

8 ounces sliced fresh wild mushrooms such as shitake, portobello, or chanterelle

2 dried porcini mushrooms, rehydrated and chopped

1 teaspoon chopped fresh thyme

Beat milk, eggs and salt in a medium bowl. Add bread and dressing. Cover and let dish stand at room temperature about 30 minutes or until bread has absorbed the milk mixture. Press any bread that is not moist into the liquid.

Heat olive oil in 9-inch skillet and add fresh mushrooms. Cook over medium-high heat until tender and liquid has evaporated. Add the porcini and thyme. Cool slightly and add to bread mixture.

Heat oven to 350°F with oven rack in middle. Lightly spray 9 x 9-inch baking dish with nonstick cooking spray. Add the bread mixture to the prepared dish.

Bake 30 to 40 minutes or until set in the center and a knife inserted near center comes out clean although it will be wet. Cool slightly and serve warm.

> BAKER'S NOTES: Any fresh mushrooms will work here. Sliced cremini mushrooms don't add as much flavor but work very well when combined with a couple of porcinis.
>
> Fresh thyme goes well with the meaty flavors of the mushrooms. Strip the leaves from the stem and chop slightly. You can add ¼ teaspoon dried thyme leaves instead.

meDITeRRanean sTRaTa

Brunch is one of my favorite times to entertain friends and family, and this hearty brunch casserole brimming with sunny flavors from the south of France is always a hit. Because it can be refrigerated overnight, it can be in the oven as the guests arrive.

MAKES 8 TO 12 SERVINGS

6 English muffins, split and cubed

12 ounces drained, cooked Italian sausage

1 (14-ounce) can extra-small artichokes, drained and quartered

½ cup chopped roasted red pepper

¼ cup Kalamata olives or ripe olives, pitted and sliced

1 ½ cups shredded Provolone cheese

4 ounces feta cheese, crumbled

3 cups whole milk

8 eggs, beaten

2 tablespoons basil pesto

½ teaspoon coarse salt

Lightly spray 13 x 9-inch baking dish with nonstick cooking spray.

Arrange muffin cubes in bottom of baking dish. Crumble sausage over muffins and top with artichokes, red pepper, olives, Provolone cheese, and feta cheese.

Beat milk, eggs, pesto, and salt until blended in large bowl and pour over other ingredients. Using a spoon, press ingredients down into the liquid. Cover with plastic wrap and refrigerate overnight.

Heat oven to 350°F with oven rack in middle. Uncover the casserole.

Bake 40 to 50 minutes or until set and a knife inserted near center comes out clean although it will be wet.

Letting the dish sit for 5 to 10 minutes before cutting makes it easier to serve. Cover and refrigerate any remaining.

BAKER'S NOTE: You can let the dish stand at room temperature about ½ hour until the milk is absorbed if you don't want to make it the day before serving.

SECRETS TO SUCCESS: I like the texture of English muffins, but cubed French bread or other chewy bread creates variety.

Unless you make your own pesto with fresh basil from the garden, purchase it already prepared. You can also purchase roasted red peppers in a jar.

oven-baked french toast

We call it French toast, but the French refer to it as "pain perdu," which literally translates as lost bread. It refers to day-old French bread transformed into a familiar breakfast treat. Serve it simply with maple syrup or caramel sauce or sprinkle it generously with powdered sugar and top with fresh berries. I have also served it with New Orleans Praline Sauce (see page 286).

MAKES 6 TO 8 SERVINGS

> 12 slices (1-inch-thick) French bread
> 6 eggs
> 2 tablespoons sugar
> ¼ teaspoon salt
> 1 teaspoon vanilla
> 3 cups milk

Arrange bread in a lightly greased 13 x 9-inch baking dish.

Beat eggs, sugar, salt, and vanilla in large bowl until blended. Beat in milk and stir well.

Pour milk mixture over bread, pushing the slices into the milk. Cover and refrigerate overnight or at least 2 hours. Uncover before baking.

Heat oven to 350°F with oven rack in middle.

Bake 35 to 45 minutes until lightly browned and puffed, and a knife inserted near the center comes out clean although it will be wet. Serve at once.

> SECRETS TO SUCCESS: This doesn't need to be prepared the day before, but allow enough time for the bread to absorb the milk.

CHOCOLATE BREAD PUDDING WITH CUSTARD SAUCE

Chocolate bread pudding combines two of my favorite flavors: chocolate and custard. Bread pudding is very popular in New Orleans and is served with a custard-based sauce generously spiked with bourbon or straight whiskey.

MAKES 8 SERVINGS

> 1 cup whipping cream
> 6 ounces semisweet chocolate, chopped
> ½ cup sugar
> Pinch of salt
> 4 eggs
> 1 cup milk
> 1 teaspoon vanilla
> 6 cups 1-inch pieces of day-old bread
> Custard Sauce (see page 284)

Heat whipping cream in small saucepan over medium heat until it begins to simmer. Add chocolate and remove from heat. Let stand until chocolate melts, stirring once or twice. Cool slightly

Beat sugar, salt, and eggs in medium bowl until mixture is completely smooth. Stir in milk and vanilla. Add chocolate mixture and mix well.

Place bread in lightly greased 9-inch pie pan. Pour milk mixture over bread and let dish stand about 1 hour. Push any bread not moistened down into the milk.

Heat oven to 325°F with oven rack in middle.

Bake 35 to 40 minutes or until set and a knife inserted near center comes out clean although it will be wet.

Cool on wire cooling rack until serving, or cool to room temperature and refrigerate. Cut into wedges and serve with Custard Sauce.

> BAKER'S NOTE: Adding the chocolate to hot cream is an easy way to melt it quickly without burning it.
>
> SECRETS TO SUCCESS: I prefer chocolate squares and not chocolate chips for melting because the squares melt more smoothly.
>
> Add 2 tablespoons of bourbon to the Custard Sauce for an adult treat.

WHITE CHOCOLATE CRèME BRULéE

Many restaurants are famous for their Crème Brulée, or Burnt Cream. Unfortunately for home cooks, they have special equipment to create the crispy sugar topping. Caramelizing can be done efficiently under the broiler or with a kitchen torch. If this is an irresistible dessert you plan to fix often, invest in a kitchen torch.

MAKES 6 SERVINGS

1 cup whipping cream
1 cup half-and-half
4 egg yolks
3 tablespoons sugar + more for caramelizing
3 ounces white chocolate, coarsely chopped

Heat oven to 325°F with oven rack in middle.

Combine whipping cream and half-and-half in small saucepan. Heat over medium heat until mixture simmers. Cool to lukewarm.

Beat egg yolks and sugar in medium bowl until blended. Slowly stir cream mixture into yolk mixture.

Divide white chocolate into 6 crème brulée dishes. Pour cream mixture through a wire mesh strainer into each dish. Place dishes in 13 x 9-inch baking dish. Add hot water to a level of about ½ inch.

Bake 28 to 33 minutes or until just set and a knife inserted near center comes out clean although it will be wet.

Let stand at room temperature until cool. Cover and refrigerate at least 4 hours. Desserts must be well chilled before creating the topping.

Blot tops with paper towel to absorb any liquid. Sift about 1 tablespoon sugar onto each ramekin. Caramelize with a kitchen torch (or broil).

To broil, heat broiler to high and place oven rack as close as possible to the heat. Place desserts on a tray and broil about 2 minutes.

Serve desserts within 1 hour of caramelizing for a crackly top.

BAKER'S NOTE: Crème brulée dishes are wide and shallow, but you can also use custard cups or ramekins. The baking time will increase slightly. The custards are done when a knife inserted near center comes out clean although it will be wet.

SECRETS TO SUCCESS: Sift a thin, even layer of sugar over the custards to create the topping. Watch carefully when you use the broiler because the sugar melts all at once and can burn easily.

PUMPKIN CRÈME

Try this dessert for Thanksgiving instead of pumpkin pie. It provides all the traditional pie flavors but can be made the day before. That means one less thing happening in the kitchen before the big meal. Serve the squares with a little caramel sauce and a dollop of whipped cream.

MAKES 9 SERVINGS

¾ cup sugar

¼ cup water

¼ teaspoon lemon juice or distilled vinegar

CUSTARD

1 cup canned pumpkin (from a 15-ounce can)

¾ cup sugar

⅓ cup pure maple syrup

3 eggs, beaten

1 teaspoon cinnamon

¼ teaspoon ground ginger

⅛ teaspoon salt

1 (12-ounce) can evaporated 2% milk

Heat oven to 325°F with oven rack in center.

Cook sugar, water, and lemon juice in heavy saucepan over medium-high heat until sugar is dissolved. Swirl pan a few times to wash down sides. Reduce heat to low and cook, swirling pan occasionally, until syrup becomes a deep golden color, about 6 minutes.

Carefully pour syrup into 8 x 8-inch baking dish. Tilt dish to spread syrup evenly. Be careful, as dish and saucepan will be very hot.

Combine pumpkin, sugar, maple syrup, eggs, cinnamon, ginger, and salt in large bowl. Beat with whisk until smooth. Gradually stir in milk.

Pour pumpkin mixture into prepared baking dish. Place baking dish in larger pan and set on oven rack. Pour hot water into larger pan to a depth of about ½ inch.

Bake 45 to 55 minutes or until set in center and a knife inserted near center comes out clean although it will be wet. Remove baking dish from the water bath and cool on wire rack. Cover and refrigerate overnight.

Cut into squares to serve and spoon some caramel sauce over top. A little whipped cream is usually expected at Thanksgiving!

BAKER'S NOTE: Because the sugar syrup becomes very hot when it is caramelized, you need to use care in handling the pan and the dish.

SECRET TO SUCCESS: I recommend pure maple syrup for the best flavor but pancake syrup is a good substitute.

Using a water bath helps the custard bake evenly. Be careful with the water, as it is very hot. Don't let your potholder get wet.

chapter eight

cheesecakes

MANY COOKBOOKS PLACE CHEESECAKES in the cakes chapter, but I think they deserve a chapter of their own. Most of the techniques needed for perfect cheesecake are unique to this dessert. Baking cheesecake is about baking with eggs and knowing when to stop. Although made from a short list of ingredients, baking perfect cheesecakes requires a little practice. When cheesecakes are overbaked, they will crack, so the goal is to prevent cracking. Cracks affect appearance only and are easily corrected when the cake is cut or heaped with fresh fruit.

Slightly sweet and velvety smooth cheesecake is the ideal showcase for different flavors, and I've included a few of my favorites here. Begin with a quality cream cheese, such as Philadelphia brand, and never use reduced-fat products unless specified in the recipe. Only use solid, not whipped cream cheese, which already has air whipped into it. As with all baking, use the best chocolate you can find, pure vanilla extract, and fresh citrus. Have all the ingredients at room temperature by removing them about 1 hour before you start to bake.

Beat the cream cheese until it is smooth and creamy before adding the sugar. If there are lumps in the cream cheese and sugar mixture, they will not disappear later. (As a last resort, you can strain the batter before pouring it into the crust.) Beat in the eggs, one at a time, just until blended. Overbeating and overbaking can be a cause of cracks. Don't open the oven door until the baking time is almost up, as the cold air can cause cracking.

The cheesecake is done when it is set, except for a small area in the center about the size of a silver dollar that is still jiggly. The cake should be removed from the oven at this point because it will continue to cook for awhile and will be firm after chilling. I suggest that if you aren't sure it is set, remove it from the oven anyway. If you take it out too soon, the center may be a little soft after chilling, but that is better than dry and overbaked. Don't test by inserting a knife in the center because this will cause a crack as the cheesecake cools.

Use a springform pan, and lightly spray the sides of the pan. After baking, run a metal spatula around the edge to loosen the cheesecake, but do not release the sides. Cool to room temperature, then refrigerate. After chilling, remove the sides but leave the cheesecake on the bottom of the pan. Trying to remove the cheesecake from the pan bottom is a recipe for disaster.

Chill your cheesecake as the recipe directs, uncovered to prevent condensation from forming. Dip a sharp knife in hot water and wipe dry before cutting slices. The simplest way to serve silky smooth cheesecake is with fresh berries—no other garnish is needed.

An accurate baking temperature is always important in baking, but a wrong oven temperature when baking cheesecakes (and cakes of all kinds) can do the most damage. Check your oven with an oven thermometer and adjust as needed. Allow the oven to heat for about a half hour before baking.

A heavy-duty mixer with the paddle attachment makes beating easy, but a hand-held mixer can also do the job. You will just need to beat a little longer. Almost all cheesecake recipes call for a springform pan, and 9-inch is the most common size. Double check to be sure the bottom in attached properly. I recently tried a cheese-cake pan—an aluminum baking pan with straight 3-inch sides and a removable bottom—and now I use it all the time. It makes it easier to remove the cheesecake and cut beautiful slices.

TRADITIONAL VANILLA CHEESECAKE

Cheesecake has always been one of my family's favorite desserts. The first year my son was in college, we brought him this cheesecake when my husband and I went for Parents' Weekend. Cheesecakes are infamous because they can crack in the middle. Follow these directions carefully, and your cheesecake shouldn't crack; even if it does, once it's cut, no one else will ever know.

MAKES 8 TO 10 SERVINGS

CRUST

1 ½ cups graham cracker crumbs
⅓ cup sugar
¼ cup butter, melted

FILLING

3 (8-ounce) packages cream cheese, softened
1 cup sugar
3 eggs, room temperature
1 teaspoon vanilla

TOPPING

1 cup sour cream, room temperature
1 tablespoon sugar
1 teaspoon vanilla
Fresh berries, if desired

Heat oven to 350°F with oven rack in middle. Lightly grease sides of a 9-inch springform pan.

CRUST

Combine graham cracker crumbs, sugar, and melted butter in a medium bowl. Press crumbs into bottom and slightly up sides of the prepared pan.

FILLING

Beat cream cheese in bowl of a heavy-duty mixer on Medium speed until creamy and free of lumps. Scrape down sides of bowl. Gradually add 1 cup sugar, scraping sides of bowl occasionally, and beat until smooth.

Reduce mixer speed to Low, and add eggs, one at a time, scraping sides of bowl after each egg is added. Add vanilla and beat just until smooth. Pour batter into crust and smooth the top.

Bake 38 to 43 minutes or until cake edge is set and center (about 2-inch diameter) still jiggles. Remove cheesecake from oven and increase oven temperature to 375°F. Let cheesecake sit in pan on top of oven 5 minutes.

TOPPING

Combine sour cream, sugar, and vanilla in a small bowl. Gently drop topping onto cheesecake and spread with a metal spatula. As topping warms, it will be easier to spread. Return cheesecake to oven for 5 minutes. After removing cheesecake from oven, run a small metal spatula around the edge to help prevent cracks.

Cheesecakes need to be cooled slowly. I place them on top of the oven for about 30 minutes and then let them cool to room temperature before refrigerating. Plan to refrigerate for at least 4 hours.

To serve, release sides of springform pan and place cheesecake on serving plate (it will still be on the pan bottom). Dip a knife in warm water and wipe dry before cutting slices. Garnish with fresh berries.

BAKER'S NOTES: Always use a high-quality cream cheese like Philadelphia brand and soften it at room temperature. The eggs should be at room temperature also.

The key to making a cheesecake is baking it properly. If you are uncertain when it's done, I suggest you remove it. It will become firmer in the center when it's chilled.

SECRETS TO SUCCESS: I always purchase ready-made graham cracker crumbs to save time and ensure consistency.

savory blue cheese cheesecake

Aside from its pungent flavor and aroma, I like this appetizer cheesecake because I can make it ahead, and it keeps several days in the refrigerator. Try it with a strong-flavored blue cheese such as Danish blue or Gorgonzola cheese. Sprinkle with walnuts just before serving.

MAKES 12 TO 15 SERVINGS

1 tablespoon butter, melted
1 tablespoon dried breadcrumbs
2 (8-ounce) packages cream cheese, softened
2 eggs, room temperature
1 cup sour cream, divided
¼ teaspoon salt
4–8 drops hot pepper sauce
¼ cup chopped green onions
4 ounces blue cheese, crumbled
½ cup chopped toasted walnuts
Crackers, rye crackers, apples
Grapes for garnish, if desired

Heat oven to 325°F with oven rack in middle. Brush bottom and slightly up sides of a 7- or 8-inch springform pan with melted butter and sprinkle with breadcrumbs.

Add cream cheese to bowl of a food processor and pulse briefly until smooth. Scrape down sides of bowl and add eggs, ½ cup sour cream, salt, and hot pepper sauce. Process 15 seconds or until mixed. Add green onions and blue cheese and pulse several times. There should still be small chunks of blue cheese in mixture.

Pour batter into springform pan and smooth the top. Bake 30 to 40 minutes or until there is only an area of about 1 inch diameter in center that jiggles. Remove from oven and let cheesecake sit for 5 minutes. Spread remaining ½ cup sour cream over top, using a light touch. Return cheesecake to oven for 5 minutes or until sour cream is set.

Run a small metal spatula around cake edge to release sides. Cheesecakes need to be cooled slowly. I place them on top of the oven for about 30 minutes and then let them cool to room temperature on wire rack before refrigerating. Plan to refrigerate for at least 4 hours.

To serve, release sides of springform pan and place cheesecake on serving plate (it will still be on the pan bottom). Sprinkle cheesecake with toasted walnuts before serving. Bring cheesecake to room temperature for about an hour before serving. Serve with crackers and apple slices.

BAKER'S NOTES: Place the walnuts on a small baking pan and toast in a 350°F oven for 7 to 9 minutes. Watch nuts carefully as they can burn very quickly. Cool completely.

I like to prepare a cheese board with 2 wedges of blue cheesecake, one or two other-than-blue cheeses, and some grapes.

You can use a decorative 9-inch pie plate instead of a springform pan. Bake 25 minutes before adding the sour cream topping. Bake 5 minutes longer and cool. I've used a decorative 9-inch pie plate and served directly from it.

BLACK AND WHITE CHEESECAKE

I love this cheesecake because the vanilla filling hides beneath the chocolate until the slice is cut. Buy chocolate cookie crumbs ready-made in the baking section of the supermarket. I like to place a few raspberries and mint leaves on the serving plate.

SERVES 8 TO 10

2 ounces semisweet chocolate, chopped

CRUST

1 cup chocolate cookie crumbs

3 tablespoons sugar

¼ cup butter, melted

FILLING

3 (8-ounce) packages cream cheese, softened

1 cup sugar

3 eggs, room temperature

⅓ cup whipping cream

1½ teaspoons vanilla

GARNISH

1 ounce semisweet chocolate, for garnish

Melt chocolate in medium bowl set over, not in, simmering water, stirring occasionally. Cool slightly and reserve.

Heat oven to 350°F with oven rack in middle.

CRUST

Combine cookie crumbs, sugar, and melted butter in a medium bowl. Press crumbs into bottom and slightly up sides of a 9-inch springform pan.

FILLING

Beat cream cheese in bowl of a heavy-duty mixer on Medium speed until creamy and free of lumps. Scrape down sides of bowl. Gradually add sugar, scraping sides of bowl occasionally, and beat until smooth.

Reduce mixer speed to Low and add eggs, one at a time, scraping down sides of bowl after each egg is added.

Beat in whipping cream and vanilla. Remove about 1 ½ cups of filling and pour it into the crust. Beat the reserved melted chocolate into remaining batter. Spread the chocolate filling over the white filling, using an offset spatula. Spread chocolate to the edges, covering the white filling.

Bake 40 minutes or until edge is set and center (about 2 inches diameter) still jiggles. Cheesecake will continue to bake after it is removed from oven.

After removing cheesecake from oven, run a small metal spatula around cake edge to prevent cracks. Cool to room temperature on wire cooling rack before refrigerating. Refrigerate cheesecake at least 4 hours.

Grate the chocolate for the garnish by pulling a vegetable peeler along its sides or rub it against a metal grater. To make chocolate curls, you need a larger piece of chocolate. Garnish cheesecake with chocolate.

To serve, release sides of springform pan and cut into slices (it will still be on the pan bottom).

CHOCOLATE CHIP MINI-CHEESECAKES

Mini chocolate chips are perfect for these individual cheesecakes—there's a chip in every bite. I like to serve these with a small dollop of whipped cream and a strawberry on top of each. Save some time and take advantage of whipped cream in an aerosol can.

MAKES 12 MINI-CHEESECAKES

CRUST

1 cup chocolate cookie crumbs

3 tablespoons sugar

¼ cup butter, melted

FILLING

2 (8-ounce) packages cream cheese, softened

¾ cup sugar

2 eggs, room temperature

¼ cup whipping cream

1 teaspoon vanilla

¼ cup semisweet chocolate mini chips

Heat oven to 350°F with oven rack in middle. Line 12 cups in a standard muffin pan with foil baking cups.

CRUST

Combine cookie crumbs, sugar, and melted butter in a medium bowl. Press about 1 tablespoon of mixture into each baking cup. There will be about 2 tablespoons remaining to use after baking.

FILLING

Beat cream cheese in bowl of a heavy-duty mixer on Medium speed until creamy and free of lumps. Scrape down sides of bowl. Gradually add sugar, scraping sides of bowl occasionally, and beat until smooth.

Reduce mixer speed to Low and add eggs, one at a time, scraping sides of bowl after each. Add whipping cream and vanilla. Stir in chocolate morsels.

Fill each baking cup with about ¼ cup filling. They will be almost full.

Bake 17 to 20 minutes or until set. The cheesecakes will be lightly browned and puffed. Sprinkle each with about ½ teaspoon of remaining cookie crumb crust.

Cool completely on wire cooling rack before refrigerating. These treats are better after they are refrigerated several hours or overnight.

> BAKER'S NOTES: You must use the aluminum foil baking cups with paper inserts because they are strong enough to support the cheesecakes. They are available in the baking section of supermarkets.
>
> You can substitute vanilla wafers for the chocolate cookie crumbs if you prefer.

grand marnier cheesecake

Grand Marnier gives a sophisticated flavor to this dessert that is definitely worth the expense, but any orange liqueur or orange juice are good substitutes. Use any shortbread cookie for the crust. I've also made this with a graham cracker crust. Because of the reduced-fat cream cheese, this cheesecake is a little softer than most but still very creamy.

MAKES 8 TO 12 SERVINGS

CRUST

1 ½ cups shortbread cookie crumbs
3 tablespoons butter, melted

FILLING

2 (8-ounce) packages reduced-fat cream cheese, softened
1 (8-ounce) package cream cheese, softened
1 ¼ cups sugar
4 egg whites, room temperature
2 tablespoons all-purpose flour
1 tablespoon grated orange rind
2 tablespoons Grand Marnier liqueur or orange juice
1 teaspoon vanilla

TOPPING

1 cup sour cream, room temperature
2 tablespoons sugar
1 tablespoon Grand Marnier

Heat oven to 350°F with oven rack in middle.

CRUST

Combine cookie crumbs and melted butter in a medium bowl. Press crumbs into bottom and slightly up sides of a 9-inch springform pan. Bake 8 minutes or until slightly browned.

FILLING

Beat cream cheese in bowl of a heavy-duty mixer on Medium speed until creamy and free of lumps. Scrape down sides of bowl. Gradually add sugar, scraping down sides of bowl occasionally, and beat until smooth.

Reduce mixer speed to Low and add egg whites, one at a time, scraping down sides of bowl after each addition. Add flour, orange rind, Grand Marnier, and vanilla and beat until smooth. Pour into prepared pan and smooth the top.

Bake 38 to 43 minutes or until cake edge is set and center (about 2 inches diameter) still jiggles. Remove cheesecake from oven and increase oven temperature to 375°F. Let cheesecake sit in pan on top of oven 5 minutes.

TOPPING

Combine sour cream, sugar, and Grand Marnier in a small bowl. Gently drop the topping onto the cheesecake and spread with a spatula. Return cheesecake to oven for 5 minutes.

After removing cheesecake from oven, run a small metal spatula around cake edge so cheesecake doesn't crack as it cools.

Cool completely in pan on wire cooling rack and then refrigerate at least 4 hours before cutting. To serve, release sides of springform pan and cut into slices (it will still be on the pan bottom). I like to use orange slices as a garnish.

BAKER'S NOTE: An easy way to make cookie crumbs is to put the cookies in a food storage bag and zip it closed. Use your rolling pin to crush the cookies.

SECRETS TO SUCCESS: The orange peel gives this cheesecake a distinctive flavor. Don't omit it.

CHOCOLATE PECAN CHEESECAKE

This is a special-occasion cheesecake, with its nutty crust and silky chocolate filling. Use a high-quality chocolate such as Scharffen Berger or Callebaut, as the creamy texture of this cheesecake will accent the deep chocolate flavor.

SERVES 12 TO 16

6 ounces bittersweet chocolate, chopped

CRUST

1¾ cups ground pecans (about 6 ounces)
¼ cup all-purpose flour
2 tablespoons sugar
3 tablespoons butter, melted

FILLING

3 (8-ounce) packages cream cheese, softened
¾ cup sugar
3 eggs, room temperature
3 tablespoons all-purpose flour
½ cup whipping cream
1½ teaspoons vanilla

Melt chocolate in medium bowl set over, not in, simmering water, stirring occasionally. Cool slightly and reserve.

Heat oven to 350°F with oven rack in middle. Grease sides of a 9-inch springform pan.

CRUST

Combine pecans, flour, sugar, and melted butter in a medium bowl and press into bottom and slightly up sides of the prepared pan. Bake 8 to 10 minutes or until pecans are toasted.

FILLING

Beat cream cheese in bowl of a heavy-duty mixer on Medium speed until creamy and free of lumps. Scrape down sides of bowl. Gradually add sugar, scraping down sides of bowl occasionally, and beat until smooth.

Reduce mixer speed to Low and add eggs, one at a time, scraping down sides of bowl after each. Add flour and beat until smooth. Beat in whipping cream, reserved chocolate, and vanilla and pour into crust, smoothing the top.

Bake 37 to 43 minutes or until cake edge is set and center (about 2 inches diameter) still jiggles.

After removing cheesecake from oven, run a small metal spatula around cake edge so cheesecake doesn't crack as it cools. Cool completely in pan on cooling rack, and then refrigerate several hours before cutting.

To serve, release sides of springform pan and cut into slices (it will still be on the pan bottom). Garnish with whipped cream.

BAKER'S NOTES: For this cheesecake, I grind the pecans in my food processor. Don't process too long or the nuts will turn into a spread.

Remove the cheesecake from the refrigerator about 1 hour before serving for the best flavor and texture. To cut, dip a knife into hot water and wipe dry before using.

SECRETS TO SUCCESS: For a lovely garnish, dip pecan halves into melted chocolate. Let stand at room temperature until the chocolate is set.

chapter nine

BUTTER CAKES, POUND CAKES, AND ANGEL FOOD CAKES

EVERY CELEBRATION STARTS with a cake: a birthday cake, a wedding cake, a cake to welcome new neighbors, and nothing compares with the tender, buttery richness of a homemade cake. Just follow these recipes, pay attention to details and you'll be proud to serve a fine-textured cake made from scratch. All baking involves chemistry and technique, and nowhere is this as critical as in successful cake baking.

BUTTER CAKES

There are two types of cakes: butter cakes and foam cakes. Butter cakes include basic cakes and pound cakes and contain a high proportion of butter, sugar, and eggs. Although some recipes use solid vegetable shortening, butter is preferred for most cakes because of its flavor. While most butter cakes contain baking powder, some pound cakes are lightened only by the air beaten into the batter.

Creaming the butter and sugar thoroughly before and after adding the eggs is the most important step in baking a butter cake, as it creates the tiny pockets of air that expand with the steam created in baking, causing the cake to rise. The more air that is beaten into the butter mixture, the lighter the cake will be. Butter, eggs, and milk should all be at room temperature for the best results. If the ingredients are cold and the batter curdles, it affects the texture of the cake because the liquids and flour are not absorbed as well.

Unlike all-purpose flour that is sifted during processing, cake flour needs to be sifted. Sifting the dry ingredients also adds a little more air and ensures that the baking powder is evenly mixed. Add the flour in three steps, alternating with the liquid.

This preserves the lightness of the batter and enables the butter mixture to absorb the ingredients completely. Scrape down the sides of the bowl often during mixing.

angel food cakes

Angel food, or foam, cakes rise due to the air beaten into egg whites. The volume of egg whites can increase as much as six to eight times when the whites are beaten properly. Angel food cake is an American creation and is popular because it is low in calories and has no fat or cholesterol. Served with fresh sliced berries and a little whipped cream, it's a heavenly dessert.

An angel food cake is baked in an ungreased tube pan that allows the cake to rise high by clinging to the sides of the pan. Only egg whites are used in an angel food cake. Separate the whites from the yolks when the eggs are cold so that no yolk sneaks in with the whites. Even the slightest amount of egg yolk reduces the volume of the whites and thus the cake. For maximum volume, allow the egg whites to come to room temperature before beating.

When you are separating the yolks from the whites, break the egg into a small cup before you separate it. This way, if the yolk breaks, you can use the egg somewhere else. Have extra eggs on hand just in case.

Fold in the flour mixture by hand, ⅓ at a time. Swipe a rubber spatula across the top of the whites parallel to the counter and slide it down the back of the bowl. Continue this circular motion until all the flour is folded in. Rotate the bowl about a quarter turn after each fold.

cake technique

Use the correct pan size because this affects the baking time. If the wrong size pan is used, the batter won't fill it properly and the cake will either be flat and dry or overflow the pan. The pan should be filled about half full. I always allow my oven to preheat about a half hour before baking cakes.

To grease and flour a pan, spread about 1 tablespoon of solid vegetable shortening over the bottom and slightly up the sides. Add 1 to 2 tablespoons of flour, and shake the pan until it is well coated with flour. Shake out any remaining flour. I have also had good luck with the nonstick spray developed for baking, which contains flour.

Lining the bottom of the pan with parchment paper or waxed paper allows the cake to come out easily and is a wise choice for layer cakes. If you use dark baking pans, reduce the oven temperature about 25°F, as dark pans bake faster. The baking time will remain the same.

It is easy to judge the doneness of a cake by testing with a wooden skewer or toothpick. It should come out clean. The cake will also spring back when lightly touched with a finger. Use both methods to ensure success. Check for doneness one to two minutes before baking time is up. The cake layers should be cooled about 10 minutes for the structure to set before removing them from the pans and placing them on cooling racks. Before frosting, the cake will need to cool completely to room temperature, which takes about 3 hours, so plan accordingly.

Serve homemade cakes within a couple of days of baking because they have no preservatives and don't keep as long as cakes made from a mix. Store cakes at room temperature unless they have cream cheese or whipped cream in the frosting or filling, in which case they need to be refrigerated. Cake layers can be frozen for several months. Wrap unfrosted cakes with plastic wrap and foil or freezer wrap to protect the cake from drying out, and frost after thawing at room temperature.

equipment

Baking temperature is critical and is best monitored with an oven thermometer. These thermometers can be purchased inexpensively at most supermarkets.

You will need several baking pans as you practice making cakes from scratch. Round aluminum pans with vertical sides (8- or 9-inch) are used for layer cakes so you will need at least two. A 13 x 9-inch baking pan is essential. Muffin pans and mini-muffin pans are needed to make cupcakes. A nonstick fluted cake pan with a tube in the center (a Bundt pan) and a 10-inch tube pan with a removable bottom are used for specialty cakes. An angel food cake pan with a removable bottom makes it easier to remove cakes.

A heavy-duty mixer simplifies making the batter, but a small portable mixer works too—you just need to beat longer. A flour sifter, parchment paper, and a cake tester make baking easier, but you can use a fine mesh strainer, waxed paper, and a tooth-pick or bamboo skewer just as well. An offset metal spatula is helpful for frosting cakes and cupcakes.

HOW TO BAKE AND FROST A LAYER CAKE

The first step to a fabulous layer cake occurs before baking: preheat the oven for at least 30 minutes at the baking temperature while you prepare the batter. Prepare two 8- or 9-inch baking pans as directed in the recipe. Divide the batter equally between the pans. For an easy way to measure this, stand a knife upright in each pan and compare batter depth. Adjust the levels if there is a noticeable difference.

Do not open the oven door until the baking time is almost up. Cool the cakes 10 minutes on a wire cooling rack before removing them from the pans. To remove the cakes from the pans, run a small metal spatula around the edges, loosening the sides of the cake. Place a wire rack over the top of the cake and carefully invert so that the cake falls onto the rack. If you have lined the bottom of the pan with paper, remove it and turn the cake right side up, using a second rack. Cool completely.

After the cake is completely cool, brush the crumbs off the sides, using a pastry brush or your fingers. Removing most of the crumbs makes it much easier to spread the frosting. Place one layer bottom up on a serving plate. I have found that it is best to use a flat plate, not a dinner plate that slopes.

Spread the top of the layer with about 1 cup of frosting. Cover with the second layer, right side up. Spread a thin layer of frosting around the sides of the cake, sealing in any remaining crumbs. This is called a crumb coat and makes it easier to spread the frosting on the top and sides. Finish with decorative swirls.

BASIC BUTTER CAKE

Every birthday celebration starts with a cake, and my family's memories begin with this classic cake. The critical step in cake baking is called "creaming"— beating the butter, sugar, and eggs thoroughly— which adds air to the batter and makes a tender crumb. I usually frost this cake with Creamy Chocolate Frosting (see page 280).

MAKES 2 (9-inch) LAYERS

2 ¼ cups cake flour
1 tablespoon baking powder
½ teaspoon salt
½ cup unsalted butter, softened
1 ¼ cups sugar
2 eggs, room temperature
1 teaspoon vanilla
1 cup milk, room temperature

Heat oven to 350°F with rack in middle. Using the bottom edge of a 9-inch round cake pan, draw 2 circles on parchment paper or waxed paper. Cut out and place one circle in the bottom of each cake pan. Grease halfway up the sides of both pans.

Sift the cake flour, baking powder, and salt into a medium bowl.

Beat butter in bowl of a heavy-duty mixer on Medium speed until creamy. Gradually add sugar, scraping sides of bowl occasionally, and beat 2 minutes. Beat in eggs, one at a time, scraping sides of bowl after each egg is added. Add vanilla and continue beating for 2 minutes until mixture is very light and creamy.

Reduce mixer speed to Low. Add flour mixture in 3 additions, alternating with 2 additions of milk. Scrape down bowl after each addition. Beat until smooth, but no longer than 15 seconds. Pour into prepared pans and spread evenly.

Bake 25 to 30 minutes or until a toothpick inserted in center of cake comes out clean and cake springs back when touched lightly. Cakes will be light golden brown and might be starting to pull away from pan sides. Cool 10 minutes on wire cooling rack.

To remove cakes from pans, run a small metal spatula around edges of pans, loosening sides of the cake. Place a wire rack over top of cake and carefully invert. Peel off the paper and turn cake right side up, using a second rack. Cool completely, about 3 hours. See How to Bake and Frost a Layer Cake (page 174).

BAKER'S NOTES: Basic Butter Cake can be baked in a greased and floured 13 x 9- inch baking pan. Bake 32 to 38 minutes or until a toothpick inserted in the center comes out clean. The cake should spring back when touched lightly. Cool completely on a wire cooling rack before frosting.

To determine if layer cake pans contain equal amounts of batter, stand a knife upright in the pans and compare the levels.

I often use unsalted butter, as I have in this cake, because of its unique flavor. If you do use unsalted butter, you still should use ½ teaspoon of salt.

SECRETS TO SUCCESS: A little solid vegetable shortening or butter in the bottom of the pan helps secure the paper.

CHOCOLATE FUDGE CAKE

A dense, fudgy chocolate cake is always popular at pot lucks or family gatherings. Using unsweetened cocoa (instead of melted chocolate) combined with buttermilk gives extra depth to the chocolate flavor in this cake. I always frost the cake with Creamy Whipped Frosting (see page 282) flavored with a little almond extract.

MAKES 13 X 9-INCH CAKE, 16 SERVINGS

2 cups all-purpose flour
¾ cup unsweetened cocoa
1½ teaspoons baking soda
½ teaspoon salt
¾ cup butter, softened
¾ cup granulated sugar
¾ cup firmly packed light brown sugar
2 eggs
1½ teaspoons vanilla
1½ cups lowfat buttermilk, room temperature

Heat oven to 350°F with rack in middle. Grease and flour bottom of a 13 x 9-inch baking pan.

Sift together flour, cocoa, baking soda, and salt.

Beat butter in bowl of a heavy-duty mixer on Medium speed until creamy. Gradually add granulated sugar and brown sugar, scraping sides of bowl occasionally, and beat 2 minutes. Beat in eggs, one at a time, scraping sides of bowl after each egg is added. Add vanilla and beat 2 minutes more until mixture is very light and creamy.

Reduce mixer speed to Low. Add flour mixture in 3 additions, alternating with 2 additions of buttermilk. Scrape down bowl after each addition. Beat until smooth, but no longer than 15 seconds. Pour into prepared pan and spread evenly.

Bake 30 to 35 minutes or until a toothpick inserted in center comes out clean and cake spring backs when touched lightly. Cool completely on wire cooling rack. Frost as desired.

BAKER'S NOTES: You can make your own "buttermilk" by placing 1 tablespoon lemon juice or distilled vinegar in a glass measuring cup and adding enough milk to make 1 ½ cups. Allow to stand 5 minutes before using.

I soften butter in the microwave set on Defrost. One stick (½ cup) takes about 30 seconds. Softened butter should yield slightly and hold an indentation when you press it with your finger. Be sure to use Defrost or you'll have a puddle of butter.

SECRETS TO SUCCESS: Cakes baked in a 13 x 9 inch baking pan are usually served from the pan. Line the bottom of the pan with parchment or waxed paper if you want to remove the cake.

CHOCOLATE CRÈME CAKE

Impress everyone when you serve this spectacular dessert. If you've never frosted a layer cake, this is the perfect place to start, as the whipped cream is easier to spread than other frosting and doesn't pick up crumbs as easily from the sides of the cake. The Irish cream liqueur adds extra flavor, although you can omit it. But don't forget the chocolate shavings.

MAKES 8 TO 10 SERVINGS

     6 ounces unsweetened chocolate, chopped
2 ½ cups cake flour
1 ¼ teaspoons baking soda
  ¼ teaspoon salt
  ½ cup butter, softened

1 cup firmly packed brown sugar

½ cup granulated sugar

3 eggs

1 teaspoon vanilla

1 cup lowfat buttermilk, room temperature

FROSTING

1 (3-ounce) package cream cheese, softened

2 cups whipping cream

⅓ cup powdered sugar

½ teaspoon vanilla

¼ cup Irish cream liqueur, divided

Shaved chocolate

Place chocolate in a medium bowl set bowl over, not in, simmering water until chocolate melts; or use a double boiler. Stir occasionally until chocolate is almost melted. Remove from heat and cool.

Heat oven to 350°F with rack in middle. Line bottoms of two 9-inch round cake pans with parchment paper and grease and flour halfway up sides.

Sift flour, baking soda, and salt into medium bowl.

Beat butter in bowl of a heavy-duty mixer on Medium speed until creamy. Gradually add brown sugar and granulated sugar and beat 2 minutes. Add eggs, one at a time, scraping down sides of bowl after each egg is added. Add vanilla and beat 2 minutes more until very light and creamy.

Reduce mixer speed to Low. Add flour mixture in 3 additions, alternating with 2 additions of buttermilk. Scrape down bowl after each addition. Beat in melted chocolate. Beat until smooth but no longer than 15 seconds. Pour batter into prepared pans and spread evenly.

Bake 28 to 33 minutes or until a toothpick inserted in center comes out clean and cake springs back when touched lightly. Cool 10 minutes on wire cooling rack.

To remove cakes from pans, run a small metal spatula around edges of pans, loosening sides of the cake. Place a wire rack over top of cake and carefully invert. Peel off paper and turn cake right side up, using a second rack. Cool completely, about 3 hours.

FROSTING

Beat cream cheese at Medium speed in bowl of a heavy-duty mixer, using whisk attachment, until smooth. Add whipping cream and beat on High speed until soft peaks form. (When you lift beaters, cream should form peaks that fold back on themselves.)

Add powdered sugar and vanilla and beat until slightly firm peaks form. Stir in 2 tablespoons liqueur.

Brush crumbs off sides of the layer cakes. Place one cake layer on a serving plate and drizzle with remaining 2 tablespoons liqueur. Spread about 1 cup whipped cream frosting on top of cake layer and cover with second layer.

Spread a thin layer of whipped cream frosting around sides of cake. Generously spread top of cake with frosting. Spread remaining frosting around the sides. Decorate cake top with shaved chocolate.

This cake must be stored in the refrigerator. Cover loosely with foil.

BAKER'S NOTES: Refer to "How to Bake and Frost a Layer Cake" on page 174 for more detailed frosting directions.

For shaved chocolate, warm a bar of semisweet chocolate with your hand. Pull a vegetable peeler down the side of the bar to create shavings.

Peach Melba Upside Down Cake

. . . .

Peach Melba was created to honor Dame Nellie Melba, an Australian opera singer. Now a classic, any dessert containing peaches and raspberries is named peach Melba. In the summer juicy ripe peaches and tangy-tart raspberries contrast with the caramelized topping and tender cake. A little whipped cream makes it complete.

MAKES 9 SERVINGS

TOPPING

¼ cup butter, melted
⅔ cup firmly packed brown sugar
2 medium peaches, peeled and sliced
1 tablespoon lemon juice
½ cup fresh raspberries

CAKE

1¼ cups all-purpose flour
1 cup sugar
1½ teaspoons baking powder
¼ teaspoon salt
½ cup butter, room temperature
2 eggs, lightly beaten
1 teaspoon almond extract

Heat oven to 350°F with rack in middle.

TOPPING

Place melted butter and brown sugar in bottom of 9 x 9-inch baking pan.

Toss peaches with lemon juice and add to pan. Add raspberries and gently poke them into the brown sugar.

cake

Combine flour, sugar, baking powder, and salt in bowl of a heavy-duty mixer. Add softened butter, eggs, and almond extract and beat on Low speed until well mixed. Scrape down sides of bowl.

Increase mixer speed to Medium and beat 2 minutes. Pour batter over the fruit.

Bake 35 to 40 minutes or until cake springs back when touched lightly. You can test with a toothpick, but only insert it into the cake. Remove cake from oven and cool 5 minutes on wire cooling rack.

You need to remove cake from pan while still warm so topping will come out easily. Loosen edges of cake with small metal spatula and cover cake with a serving plate. Carefully invert the cake onto the serving plate. If any topping remains in pan, remove with spatula and gently spread over cake.

Serve warm or at room temperature. Store cake in refrigerator.

BAKER'S NOTES: To peel the peaches, drop them into boiling water for 20 seconds. Remove with slotted spoon and drop them into cold water. The skins will slip off easily.

If you don't have a large serving plate, invert the cake, using the back of a 15 x 10-inch jellyroll pan covered with aluminum foil.

SECRETS TO SUCCESS: Because the cake is prepared using the quick or one-bowl method, the butter must be very soft. Allow the butter to sit at room temperature about 2 hours before using.

MISSISSIPPI MUD CAKE

As soon as you start mixing this cake you'll know why it is called "mud" cake. The heated cocoa, butter, oil, and water look exactly like mud. But it doesn't taste like mud—rather, it has a rich chocolate flavor and lots of sinful fudgy frosting. Because this quick cake is easy to prepare and uses basic ingredients, this is the recipe to prepare when dessert is needed at the last minute. Everyone loves it, especially kids, and the recipe makes a lot!

MAKES 30 OR MORE BARS

> 2 cups sugar
> 2 cups all-purpose flour
> ¼ teaspoon salt
> ¼ cup unsweetened cocoa
> 1 cup water
> ½ cup vegetable oil
> ½ cup butter
> ½ cup lowfat buttermilk
> 2 eggs
> 1 teaspoon vanilla
> 1 teaspoon baking soda

FROSTING

> ¼ cup unsweetened cocoa
> ½ cup butter
> ⅓ cup milk
> 3¾ cups powdered sugar
> 1 teaspoon vanilla

Heat oven to 375°F with rack in middle. Grease and flour a 15 x 10 x 1-inch jellyroll pan or spray nonstick baking spray.

Mix sugar, flour, and salt in large bowl.

Combine cocoa, water, oil, and butter in medium saucepan. Heat over medium heat, stirring constantly, until mixture comes to full boil. Reduce heat to low and simmer 1 minute. Pour over sugar mixture, and stir until well mixed.

Beat buttermilk, eggs, and vanilla in medium bowl until smooth. Stir in baking soda. Add to the flour mixture and beat until smooth. Scrape down sides of bowl and pour batter into prepared pan.

Bake 18 to 22 minutes or until a toothpick inserted in center comes out clean and cake springs back when touched with a finger.

FROSTING

Combine cocoa, butter, and milk in saucepan and bring to a boil over medium heat. Reduce heat to low and cook 1 minute. Remove from heat, add powdered sugar, and beat until smooth. Stir in vanilla. Spread frosting over the warm cake. Let cake cool completely before cutting.

> SECRETS TO SUCCESS: Start making the frosting during the last few minutes of baking so it will be ready to spread over the warm cake.

TRES LECHES CAKE

This traditional Hispanic dessert is currently very popular in the United States. Tres Leches translates as "three milks," and this cake is literally drenched in sweet milks—whipping cream, evaporated milk, and condensed milk. Whole milk is an extra! I like to serve it with a little whipped cream and mixed fresh berries.

MAKES 24 SERVINGS

2 cups all-purpose flour
2 teaspoons baking powder
¼ teaspoon salt
¾ cup butter, softened
1 ½ cups sugar
4 eggs, separated
1 teaspoon vanilla
1 cup whole milk
½ teaspoon cream of tartar

TOPPING

¾ cup whipping cream
1 (15-ounce) can sweetened condensed milk
1 (5-ounce) can evaporated milk

Heat oven to 350°F with rack in middle. Grease and flour a 13 x 9-inch baking pan.

Combine flour, baking powder, and salt in medium bowl.

Beat butter until creamy in bowl of a heavy-duty mixer on Medium speed. Gradually add sugar, scraping down sides of bowl occasionally, and beat 2 minutes. Beat in egg yolks, scrape down sides of bowl, and add vanilla. Beat 2 minutes more until mixture is very light and creamy.

Reduce mixer speed to Low. Add flour mixture in 3 additions, alternating with the whole milk in 2 additions. Scrape down sides of bowl after each addition. Beat until smooth, but no longer than 15 seconds.

Place egg whites and cream of tartar in bowl of a heavy-duty mixer fitted with the whisk. Beat on High speed until whites form soft peaks. (When you lift beaters, whites should form peaks that fall softly down.)

Add whites to batter with a folding motion. Bring a rubber spatula across the beaten whites in a motion parallel to the counter, slide the spatula down the back of the bowl, and pull it back in the other direction, lifting at the end. Rotate bowl as you fold. Pour batter into prepared pan.

Bake 30 to 35 minutes or until a toothpick inserted in center comes out clean. The cake may not be browned. Place cake pan on wire cooling rack and pierce cake generously with a fork or skewer.

TOPPING

Combine whipping cream, condensed milk, and evaporated milk in medium bowl and mix well. Spoon generously over the cake. Continue to add more liquid as topping is absorbed. You may not use it all. This cake must be stored in the refrigerator.

BAKER'S NOTES: It is easier to separate the egg yolks from the whites when the eggs are chilled. Do this about ½ hour before starting the cake.

Condensed milk has lots of sugar added, and evaporated milk does not—read the labels carefully.

SECRETS TO SUCCESS: Be sure bowl for beating egg whites is free from fat so that the whites will whip well.

CaRROT CUPCakeS WITH WHIPPeD CReam CHeeSe FROSTING

Shred the carrots in a food processor for quick results or by hand using a box grater. I tried buying shredded carrots and chopping them instead of grating, but I didn't like the result. Most carrot cakes contain oil, but once again I've used butter to lighten this treasured classic. The frosting, a combination of cream cheese and whipped cream, is lighter than other cream cheese frostings.

MAKES 24 CUPCAKES

3 cups all-purpose flour
1 teaspoon baking powder
1 teaspoon baking soda
1 teaspoon cinnamon
½ teaspoon salt
1 cup butter, softened
1 cup granulated sugar
1 cup firmly packed brown sugar
4 eggs
1 teaspoon vanilla
½ cup lowfat buttermilk
3 cups grated carrots (12 ounces)

FROSTING

1 (8-ounce) package cream cheese, softened
2 cups powdered sugar, sifted
1 teaspoon vanilla
1 cup whipping cream

Heat oven to 350°F with rack in middle. Line 24 muffin cups with paper liners.

Combine flour, baking powder, baking soda, cinnamon, and salt in medium bowl.

Beat butter in bowl of a heavy-duty mixer on Medium speed until creamy. Gradually add granulated sugar and brown sugar, scraping sides of bowl occasionally, and beat 2 minutes.

Beat in eggs, one at a time, scraping down sides of bowl after each egg is added. Add vanilla and beat 2 minutes until mixture is very light and creamy.

Reduce mixer speed to Low. Add flour mixture in 3 additions, alternating with 2 additions of buttermilk. Scrape down sides of bowl after each addition. Beat until smooth, but no longer than 15 seconds. Add carrots and mix. Pour into prepared muffin cups.

Bake 25 to 30 minutes or until a toothpick inserted in center of a cupcake comes out clean and cake springs back when touched lightly. The tops may look a little moist. Cool 5 minutes and remove from pan. Cool completely on wire cooling rack. The cupcakes must be at room temperature before frosting.

FROSTING

Place cream cheese in bowl of a heavy-duty mixer and beat at Medium speed until creamy and smooth. Add powdered sugar, vanilla, and whipping cream. Increase mixer speed to High and beat until light and fluffy, scraping down sides of bowl a few times.

Frosting should be firm enough to spread on cupcakes. After frosting cupcakes, store them in refrigerator. They can also be frozen.

BAKER'S NOTES: Buttermilk contains an acid that reacts with baking soda to release gas during baking. Purchase dried buttermilk and keep it on hand for any recipe that requires buttermilk. It keeps several months in the freezer.

If you only have one 12-cup muffin pan, make 12 cupcakes, and bake the remaining batter in a greased and floured 9-inch round cake pan. Bake 22 to 25 minutes.

To bake in a 13 x 9-inch baking pan, allow 40 to 50 minutes. Test for doneness with a toothpick.

spicy applesauce cake

After processing, dark brown sugar contains a little more molasses than light brown sugar. The extra molasses emphasizes the spicy flavors in applesauce cake. Whipped Cream Cheese Frosting (see page 281) or Buttercream Frosting (see page 280) provide the perfect finish.

MAKES 20 SERVINGS

2 cups all-purpose flour
1 teaspoon baking powder
½ teaspoon baking soda
1 teaspoon cinnamon
½ teaspoon ground ginger
½ teaspoon salt
¼ teaspoon ground allspice
½ cup butter, softened
1 cup firmly packed dark brown sugar
½ cup granulated sugar
2 eggs
1 teaspoon vanilla
1½ cups applesauce
½ cup raisins, if desired
½ cup chopped walnuts, if desired

Heat oven to 350°F with rack in middle. Grease and flour a 13 x 9-inch baking pan.

Sift flour, baking powder, baking soda, cinnamon, ginger, salt, and allspice into medium bowl.

Beat butter in bowl of a heavy-duty mixer on Medium speed until creamy. Gradually add brown sugar and granulated sugar, scraping sides of bowl occasionally, and beat 2 minutes. Beat in eggs, one at a time, scraping sides of bowl after each egg is added. Add vanilla and beat 2 minutes until mixture is very light and creamy.

Reduce mixer speed to Low. Add flour mixture in 3 additions, alternating with 2 additions of applesauce. Scrape down bowl after each addition. Beat until smooth, but no longer than 15 seconds. Stir in raisins and walnuts, if using, and pour batter into prepared pan.

Bake 30 to 38 minutes or until a toothpick inserted in center comes out clean and cake springs back when touched lightly. Cool completely on wire cooling rack before frosting.

BAKER'S NOTE: The flavors of dark brown sugar and light brown sugar are slightly different but they are interchangeable.

SECRETS TO SUCCESS: The cake will need to cool about 2 hours before frosting.

This cake freezes well because it is so moist, but be sure it's tightly wrapped.

Rather than buy a jar of applesauce, I often buy individual cups of applesauce and use only what I need.

---

vanilla bean pound cake

In colonial America, a pound cake was made using one pound each of sugar, butter, eggs, and flour. All of the leavening came from beating air into the batter, an exhausting process that is much easier today with an electric mixer. In today's version, the proportions are no longer exactly one pound and the cake contains a little baking powder. In this simple cake with uncomplicated flavors, the vanilla accent is evident in every bite.

MAKES 16 SERVINGS

2 ½ cups all-purpose flour
½ teaspoon baking powder
½ teaspoon salt
1 vanilla bean
1 cup unsalted butter, softened
2 cups sugar
4 eggs, room temperature
1 cup milk, room temperature

Heat oven to 350°F with rack in lower third. Grease and flour the bottom and about 1-inch up the sides of a 10-inch tube pan with removable bottom.

Sift flour, baking powder, and salt into medium bowl.

Cut vanilla bean in half lengthwise and scrape out the tiny seeds with the tip of your knife.

Beat butter in bowl of a heavy-duty mixer on Medium speed until creamy. Gradually add sugar, scraping down sides of bowl occasionally, and beat 2 minutes.

Beat in eggs, one at a time, scraping sides of bowl after each egg is added. Add vanilla seeds and beat 3 minutes until mixture is very light and creamy.

Reduce mixer speed to Low. Add flour mixture in 3 additions, alternating with 2 additions of milk. Scrape down bowl after each addition. Beat until smooth, but no longer than 15 seconds. Pour into prepared pan and spread evenly.

Bake 55 to 65 minutes or until a toothpick inserted in center of cake comes out clean. Cool cake completely on wire cooling rack.

Run a spatula around inside of pan to loosen the cake. While cake can be completely removed from the pan, I usually leave it on the pan bottom for support.

BAKER'S NOTES: Eggs and milk should be at room temperature. Eggs can be warmed by placing them in a bowl and covering them with warm water for about 15 minutes.

The butter should be soft enough to give slightly and show a finger imprint when pressed.

SECRETS TO SUCCESS: I find that the easiest way to pour the batter into the pan is by adding about one-third at a time, rotating the pan a quarter turn or so after each portion is poured. Lightly spread the batter until it is even.

You can substitute pure vanilla extract for the vanilla beans. Use 2 teaspoons.

When you buy vanilla beans, check to be sure that they are moist so that the tiny seeds can be scraped out easily. Place the seedless vanilla bean in a container of sugar and it will flavor the sugar.

BUTTER RUM POUND CAKE

Serve this cake on a breezy summer day with fresh strawberries and whipped cream. It makes a simple and easy dessert paired with any fresh fruit. I also bake these cakes to give to friends during the holidays, and they expect lots of rum in the glaze. The rum glaze keeps the cake moist.

MAKES 2 CAKES, 24 SERVINGS

3 cups all-purpose flour
1 teaspoon baking powder
½ teaspoon baking soda
½ teaspoon salt
1 cup butter, softened
2 cups sugar
4 eggs, room temperature
2 teaspoons vanilla
1 cup lowfat buttermilk, room temperature

GLAZE

1 cup sugar
½ cup butter
3 tablespoons water
¼ cup dark rum

Heat oven to 350°F with rack in middle. Grease and flour two 8½ x 4½-inch loaf pans and line bottoms with parchment paper.

Sift flour, baking powder, baking soda, and salt into medium bowl.

Beat butter in bowl of a heavy-duty mixer on Medium speed until creamy. Gradually add sugar, scraping sides of bowl occasionally, and beat 2 minutes. Beat in eggs, one at a time, scraping sides of bowl after each egg is added. Add vanilla and beat 2 minutes until very light and creamy.

Reduce mixer speed to Low. Add flour mixture in 3 additions, alternating with 2 additions of buttermilk. Scrape down sides of bowl after each addition. Beat until smooth, but no longer than 15 seconds. Pour batter into prepared pans.

Bake 45 to 55 minutes or until cakes are golden brown and a toothpick inserted in center comes out clean. Cakes will be starting to pull away from pan sides. Cool 5 minutes on wire cooling rack.

Run a spatula around sides of pans and lift cake bottoms slightly. Using a bamboo skewer or wooden pick, pierce tops of cakes generously so they can absorb the rum glaze.

GLAZE

Bring sugar, butter, and water to a boil over medium heat in medium saucepan, stirring often. Reduce heat to low and simmer 5 minutes. Remove pan from heat and stir in rum.

Spoon glaze generously over warm cakes, a couple of tablespoons at a time. Continue adding glaze as it is absorbed. Allow cakes to cool completely, then carefully remove them from pans.

BAKER'S NOTES: The more you pierce the cake, the more glaze it will absorb. Let the glaze soak in slowly. You may not use all of the glaze.

Use dark or gold rum. Myer's rum is a good choice because it is aged and very smooth.

SECRETS TO SUCCESS: Buttermilk can be purchased in a dried form in the baking section of your supermarket. It can be stored in the freezer and used whenever you need buttermilk for baking. Follow the directions on the package for using in recipes.

ORANGE MINI-BUNDT CAKES

Fragrant notes of citrus perfume these mini-cakes and signal a fresh orange taste in every bite. One mini-cake is a very generous serving, so I usually cut them in half. At the Holidays, two or three cakes make a lovely hostess gift, especially when presented on a holiday dish.

MAKES 6 MINI-CAKES

> 1 ½ cups all-purpose flour
> ¼ teaspoon salt
> ½ cup butter, softened
> 1 ¼ cups sugar
> 2 eggs, room temperature
> ½ teaspoon vanilla
> ½ cup whipping cream or milk, room temperature
> 1 tablespoon orange juice
> 1 tablespoon grated orange peel

GLAZE

> ¾ cup powdered sugar, sifted
> 1 tablespoon whipping cream or milk
> 1–2 tablespoons orange juice

Heat oven to 350°F with rack in middle. Thoroughly grease and flour a nonstick mini-fluted tube pan with 6 individual cups.

Sift flour and salt into medium bowl.

Beat butter in bowl of a heavy-duty mixer on Medium speed until creamy. Gradually add sugar, scraping sides of bowl occasionally, and beat 2 minutes. Beat in eggs, one at a time, scraping sides of bowl after each egg is added. Add vanilla and beat 2 minutes until the mixture is very light and creamy.

Reduce mixer speed to Low. Add flour mixture in 3 additions, alternating with 2 additions of whipping cream. Scrape down sides of bowl after each addition. Beat until smooth, but no longer than 15 seconds. Stir in orange juice and orange peel. Divide batter into prepared cups. The cups will be fairly full.

Bake 30 to 35 minutes or until a wooden pick inserted near center comes out clean. Cool on wire cooling rack 5 minutes.

Run a small metal spatula around tops of cakes, lifting to release the bottoms. To remove cakes, cover with a wire rack and invert. Cool completely.

GLAZE

Place powdered sugar, whipping cream, and orange juice in small bowl and beat until smooth. Drizzle over cakes, allowing glaze to drip down the sides.

BAKER'S NOTES: The freshly grated orange peel adds a lot of flavor, but you can use 1 teaspoon of orange extract as a substitute if you don't have a fresh orange.

It is important to grease the pan well, with shortening in the grooves, so that the cakes release easily.

SECRET TO SUCCESS: If the glaze is too thick to drizzle, add a little more juice. I place a piece of waxed paper under the cooling rack before drizzling for easy clean-up.

CHOCOLATE AMARETTO POUND CAKE

Bittersweet chocolate contains a little less sugar than semisweet and provides the perfect amount of chocolate in this rich cake. The amaretto liqueur adds a hint of almond flavor. For a stronger flavor, drizzle a powdered sugar glaze made with the liqueur over the top of the cake after spreading with the ganache. Drizzling melted white chocolate over the cake is another pretty touch.

MAKES 12 TO 16 SERVINGS

6 ounces bittersweet chocolate, chopped

2½ cups all-purpose flour

2 teaspoons baking powder

½ teaspoon salt

1 cup butter, softened

¾ cup granulated sugar

¾ cup firmly packed brown sugar

4 eggs, room temperature

2 tablespoons amaretto (almond-flavored liqueur) or 1 teaspoon almond extract

1 teaspoon vanilla

¾ cup milk

Chocolate Ganache (see page 283)

Place chocolate in a medium bowl and set bowl over, not in, simmering water until chocolate melts; or use a double boiler. Stir occasionally until chocolate is almost melted. Remove from heat and cool.

Heat oven to 350°F with rack in lower third. Spray a 10-inch fluted tube pan with nonstick baking spray with flour; or generously grease and flour the pan, getting into the grooves.

Sift flour, baking powder, and salt into medium bowl.

Beat butter in bowl of a heavy-duty mixer on Medium speed until creamy. Gradually add granulated sugar and brown sugar, scraping sides of bowl occasionally, and beat 2 minutes. Beat in eggs, one at a time, scraping sides of bowl after each egg is added. Add amaretto liqueur, vanilla, and chocolate and beat 2 minutes until mixture is very light and creamy.

Reduce mixer speed to Low. Add flour mixture in 3 additions, alternating with 2 additions of milk. Scrape down bowl after each addition. Beat until smooth, but no longer than 15 seconds. Pour into prepared pan and spread evenly.

Bake 45 to 55 minutes or until a toothpick inserted near center comes out dry. Cake will be starting to pull away from pan sides. Cool 10 minutes on wire cooling rack.

To remove cake, first run a metal spatula along sides of pan to loosen it. Place a wire cooling rack over cake and invert. Cool completely.

Prepare the Chocolate Ganache (see page 283), and pour it over top of cake, allowing it to drip down sides.

For a simple garnishing touch, just sprinkle cake with powdered sugar.

ENGLISH TRIFLE

Every Christmas Eve I serve English Trifle for dessert. It is an elegant dessert of cake, custard, sherry, and sometimes fruit. It can be made ahead, and there's usually just enough left for a quiet family dinner on Christmas. Although I only use my trifle bowl once a year, it is the centerpiece on the table, especially festive with strawberry slices arranged around the sides of the bowl.

MAKES 10 TO 12 SERVINGS

8 slices, about ½ inch thick, pound cake (purchased, or see page 191)

⅓ cup seedless raspberry jam

¼ cup cream or dry sherry

Pastry Cream (see page 285), cooled to lukewarm

1 cup sliced fresh strawberries, if desired

1 cup whipping cream

2 tablespoons powdered sugar

½ teaspoon vanilla

Whole strawberries, as garnish

Spread jam on each slice of pound cake and place in trifle bowl or in 2-quart casserole. Drizzle with sherry. Spoon Pastry Cream over pound cake. Add strawberries if desired.

Beat whipping cream in bowl of a heavy-duty mixer fitted with the whisk until soft peaks form. Add powdered sugar and vanilla and beat until thickened, scraping down sides of bowl a few times. Spread over the custard and top with whole strawberries. Refrigerate until serving.

BAKER'S NOTE: Use homemade Vanilla Bean Pound Cake (see page 191) or buy a frozen pound cake. If you bake the cake, do it a day ahead for easier slicing. After cutting the slices for the trifle, wrap the remaining cake tightly and freeze.

SECRETS TO SUCCESS: An English friend of mine gave me her recipe for trifle. She makes it with "custard powder," which is actually a cornstarch pudding mix. I like the flavor of homemade custard better, but it's less work with the mix. Custard powder can be purchased in some supermarkets or specialty stores.

angel food cake

Angel food cake probably got its name because it's lighter than air—or at least lightened by air. Just in case you break a yolk when separating the yolks and the whites, have more than one dozen eggs on hand. This heavenly cake is more difficult than most of the recipes in this book, but it teaches three important techniques: separating eggs, beating meringue, and folding ingredients together. Use some of the yolks to make Custard Sauce (see page 284) to serve with the cake.

MAKES 12 SERVINGS

1 cup cake flour
1 ½ cups sugar, divided
12 egg whites, room temperature
½ teaspoon cream of tartar
¼ teaspoon salt
1 ½ teaspoons vanilla

Heat oven to 375°F with rack in lower third.

Sift cake flour with ¾ cup of sugar into small bowl.

Place egg whites in bowl of a heavy-duty mixer fitted with the whisk. Add cream of tartar and salt and beat on Medium speed until foamy. Increase mixer speed to High and beat until soft peaks form.

Add remaining ¾ cup sugar, about 1 tablespoon at a time, while beating on High and scraping down sides of bowl occasionally. After all sugar is added, beat until stiff, glossy peaks are formed when beaters are lifted. Beat in vanilla.

By hand, fold in flour mixture, ⅓ at a time. To fold, swipe a rubber spatula across the top of the whites, parallel to the counter, and slide it down the back of the bowl. Continue this circular motion. Turn the bowl about a quarter turn after each fold. Fold until the flour disappears.

Spoon batter into ungreased 10-inch tube pan with removable bottom and spread evenly. Draw a knife through the batter to break up any large pockets of air.

Bake 30 to 40 minutes or until cake is golden brown and springs back when touched lightly. There will be cracks in the surface and they can still be slightly moist. Remove cake from oven and invert in pan until completely cool. Run spatula around sides of cake and remove sides of pan. Leave bottom of pan in place to support cake.

BAKER'S NOTE: Eggs are easier to separate if they are chilled. Be careful not to get any yolk mixed with the whites. I drop each white into a small cup before adding it to the bowl with the others just in case the yolk breaks when I crack the shell. Allow the whites to warm to room temperature before beating.

SECRETS TO SUCCESS: An angel food cake needs to cool upside down because its structure is so fragile. Some tube pans have feet to hold the cake upside down while it cools. You can also invert the pan by placing the tube over a large bottle. Experiment with this before you begin the cake.

CHOCOLATE ANGEL FOOD CAKE

Chocolate angel food cake is not quite as light as angel food because the cocoa weighs the batter down. But I love the flavor of the chocolate, especially when it's paired with almond extract. Use the chocolate cake as the base for fresh strawberries with a dollop of whipped cream.

MAKES 12 SERVINGS

¾ cup cake flour
½ cup unsweetened cocoa
1½ cups sugar, divided
12 egg whites, room temperature
½ teaspoon cream of tartar
¼ teaspoon salt
1 teaspoon vanilla
1 teaspoon almond extract

Heat oven to 375°F with rack in lower third.

Sift cake flour, cocoa, and ¾ cup sugar into small bowl.

Place egg whites in bowl of a heavy-duty mixer fitted with the whisk. Add cream of tartar and salt and beat on Medium speed until foamy. Increase mixer speed to High and beat until soft peaks form.

Add remaining ¾ cup sugar, about 1 tablespoon at a time, while beating on High and scraping down sides of bowl occasionally. After all sugar is added, beat until stiff, glossy peaks are formed when beaters are lifted. Beat in vanilla and almond extract.

By hand, fold in cocoa mixture, ⅓ at a time. To fold, swipe a rubber spatula across the top of the whites, parallel to the counter, and slide it down the back of the bowl. Continue this circular motion. Turn the bowl about a quarter turn after each fold. Fold until the flour disappears.

Spoon batter into ungreased 10-inch tube pan with removable bottom and spread evenly. Draw a knife through batter to break up any large pockets of air.

Bake 32 to 38 minutes or until cake is browned and springs back when touched lightly. The cracks on top will be dry. Remove cake from oven and invert in pan until completely cool. Run spatula around sides of cake and remove sides of pan. Leave bottom of pan in place to support cake.

BAKER'S NOTES: To judge when soft peaks have formed, turn off the mixer and lift the beaters. As you lift, the whites will be drawn up and the peaks will fold over.

Stiff glossy peaks do not fold over when the beaters are withdrawn. I also rub a little meringue between my fingers to feel if the sugar is dissolved. If I can still feel the sugar, I beat a little longer.

SECRETS TO SUCCESS: You can invert the pan by placing the tube over a large bottle. Experiment with this before you begin the cake.

chapter ten

PIES AND TARTS

HOME-BAKED APPLE PIE is one of the treasures of autumn, just as Pumpkin Pie is traditional for the winter holidays. Lemon Meringue Pie heralds the flavors of spring and Fresh Strawberry Pie smothered in whipped cream completes the annual cycle. Although everyone loves fresh pie, most bakers find it intimidating to bake one from scratch, but practicing these techniques will guarantee success.

You will understand the difference of store-bought and homemade pie crust the first time you sample a leftover scrap of dough that has been sprinkled with sugar and cinnamon and baked. As you bite into the crust, it makes a sharp snap as it shatters, and flakes of pastry float down. Making a pie crust from scratch is not difficult; it just requires following directions and using a light touch. As with any new skill, practice makes all the difference.

INGREDIENTS

The ingredients for pie pastry are basic: flour, fat, salt, and water, although there are some variations. Solid vegetable shortening is the fat many bakers prefer because it makes a tender, flaky crust. Butter adds unique flavor, but it contains some water, making it more difficult to know how much water to add, and the end result is not quite as flaky. All-purpose flour is used for most pie crusts, although pastry flour, which is lower in protein, works well but is harder to find.

While it is easy to purchase a high-quality refrigerated or frozen pie pastry, they are usually made with lard. Lard is an animal fat and is rarely used today for home baking because it can add its own unappealing flavor to the pastry. In addition, lard contains cholesterol that many people must limit in their diets.

making the crust

For a flaky pie crust, you must coat the flour with fat to prevent the formation of too much gluten, although some is necessary. Cold shortening or butter and ice water are the key. The method I find easiest and most successful for making a flaky, tender pie crust relies on a food processor because it is so fast, and the ingredients stay cool. With a processor, it's easy to cut the shortening and butter into the flour and distribute the water evenly.

After adding the fat, process only a few seconds, until the mixture resembles coarse crumbs with some pea-sized pieces. Distribute the liquid over the flour mixture and process just until the dough begins to come together. Stop the processor and pinch some pieces between your fingers to determine if a dough will form. If it is too dry, add more water, a teaspoon at a time. Gather the dough into two discs, each about 4 inches across and 1 inch high, wrap, and refrigerate at least 1 hour.

After the pastry is chilled, the butter will be firm and the gluten relaxed, making it easier to roll. When you remove the pastry from the refrigerator, allow it to stand at room temperature a few minutes if it is very firm. Because there is a high proportion of fat to flour in most recipes, you can generously dust your work surface with flour to prevent sticking.

Always roll dough from the center out to the edge, rotating the pastry after each roll. Do not use a back-and-forth motion, as that toughens the dough. By rotating as you roll, you will create a circle. Roll the dough 2 to 3 inches wider than the pie pan. If the edges are cracked, you can repair them by dabbing with a little water and then pressing them together. Once the pastry is baked, the repairs disappear.

To place the crust in the pie pan, roll it loosely onto your rolling pin and lift it. Fit it into the pie pan without stretching it, and use your fingers to press the dough into position along the bottom and sides of the pan. Spoon in the filling.

For a two-crust pie, roll out the second disc of dough 2 to 3 inches larger than the pie pan. Carefully place it over the pie filling. Press the edges of both top and bottom crusts together to seal in the filling, and flute the edges if desired. A very simple way to seal the edge after trimming excess is to press the top and bottom crusts together with the tines of a fork.

A simple way to flute the edges of crusts is to press your thumb on the outside edge of the pastry and pinch the dough around it pressing from the opposite side with two fingers of your other hand.

I like to finish the tops of my pies simply, brushing the top crust with a little milk and sprinkling it with sugar. Cut a several vents into the top to allow steam to escape. You can create fun decorations by cutting out leaves, hearts, or stars from the extra dough and placing them on top crust before baking.

Baking Techniques

Baking "blind" refers to baking the pastry without any filling. After rolling out the pastry and fitting it into the pie pan, prick it generously with a fork to prevent blistering. Chilling the dough before baking also helps it keep its shape. I line the pastry with aluminum foil and add pie weights (rice can also be used). The foil can be used to lift out the weights after the crust is partially baked. Then finish baking until the crust is browned. The weights help retain the shape of the pie shell but aren't essential.

Bake pies in the lower third of a hot oven so the bottom crust will be well browned. Fruit pies must be baked until the juices are thickened and bubbling out of the vents. If the edges of the crust begin to brown too quickly, cover them with a ring of aluminum foil. Cool pies to room temperature on a cooling rack.

Fruit pies can be stored, loosely covered, at room temperature for 1 to 2 days. Before serving they should be cooled about 2 hours. For longer storage, they should be refrigerated. Fruit pies can be reheated in a 350-degree oven for about 15 minutes. Cream or custard pies should be covered, always stored in the refrigerator, and eaten within 3 days.

Equipment

I have always used a wooden rolling pin that was my grandmother's and mother's, but there are several other kinds available. Marble keeps the dough cold, but it is very heavy, and the uneven shape of French-style rolling pins requires some practice. I use a pastry cloth and sleeve on my rolling pin, but you should experiment to see what you like best. Rolling out the dough between two pieces of parchment or waxed paper is useful if the pastry tends to stick to the rolling pin.

Pie plates and pans have slanted sides and come in several diameters, with 8-, 9-, and 10-inches being the most common. A deep-dish pie pan is usually 9- or 10- inches wide and 1½-inches deep.

Tart pans with fluted sides are used for quiches and tarts. These pans also come in several sizes. For baking individual tarts, use 3- or 4-inch pans. Metal tart pans usually have a removable bottom while porcelain and ceramic pans have solid bottoms. I recommend buying several sizes of tart and tartlet pans. The ones with removable bottoms make it easier to remove the tarts.

A food processor is the easiest way to make pie pastry, but it is not essential. A pastry blender is also a useful tool for cutting the fat into the flour when making dough by hand. Pie weights are metal or ceramic beads that prevent a crust from collapsing when it is baked blind (without a filling). For a well-browned crust, bake the pastry in the lower third of the oven. Pie shields are available: they fit over the edges of the crust to prevent excessive browning. A pie server, a triangular metal spatula, is the best way to serve a slice of pie or quiche.

BASIC PIE PASTRY

Tender and flaky pie crust is easy to make if you follow directions carefully and use a food processor. I use a combination of butter (for flavor) and shortening (for flaky tenderness). After making the dough, it should be chilled before rolling out and handled as little as possible.

PASTRY FOR 1 DOUBLE-CRUST OR 2 SINGLE-CRUST PIES

> 3 cups all-purpose flour
> ½ teaspoon salt
> ⅓ cup cold butter, cut into small cubes
> ½ cup vegetable shortening
> 6 tablespoons ice water

Place flour and salt in food processor bowl. Pulse briefly to mix. Add butter and shortening and pulse until crust resembles coarse crumbs. Pour ice water through processor tube while processor in running. Continue to process 15 to 30 seconds or until crust begins to form large clumps. If dough doesn't clump, add a little more water, 1 teaspoon at a time.

Turn pastry out onto a clean surface and gather it together. Cut in half and shape each half into a flat disc, about 5 inches across. Wrap pastry discs in plastic wrap and chill at least 1 hour. (If you only need pastry for a one-crust pie, tightly wrap the remaining disk and freeze.)

Sprinkle flour lightly on your work surface. Remove 1 pastry from refrigerator, unwrap, and dust both sides lightly with flour. Place dough in center of work surface.

Place rolling pin in center of disk and roll out dough to the edge. Rotate dough about one-quarter turn each time you roll. Roll the dough circle to an 11-inch diameter, about ⅛ inch thick. Until you've made a few pies, your circle will be ragged.

Loosely drape the crust around the rolling pin, or fold it into quarters, and lift it into a 9-inch pie pan. Unroll and press along pan edges and bottom, making sure that the pastry is not stretched. Patch if needed or trim uneven edges.

Fill pie shell or bake as directed in the recipe.

PIE PASTRY BAKED BLIND (WITHOUT FILLING)

Pastry for 9- or 10-inch single-crust pie

Roll out dough about 2 inches larger than pie pan. Place dough in pan, being careful not to stretch it. Press firmly into bottom, edges, and around top of pan. Flute edges as desired. Prick sides and bottom generously with a fork. Chill about 30 minutes.

Heat oven to 450°F with oven rack in lower third. Fill shell with pie weights wrapped in aluminum foil and bake 6 minutes. Carefully remove the weights and continue baking 3 to 6 minutes until crust is golden brown. Cool on wire cooling rack before using.

Crust can be baked without pie weights. Be sure pastry isn't stretched in the pan. Carefully press down pastry if it puffs up during baking.

BAKER'S NOTES: This recipe makes a generous amount of pastry. Each disc is more than enough to fit into a 9-inch pie pan.

If your dough sticks to the counter, gently run a thin metal spatula under the dough to release it.

To patch the pastry crust, brush the edge that needs a patch lightly with water. Cut a small piece of pastry to fit, and place it where needed. Press lightly to seal.

SECRETS TO SUCCESS: When you first begin to work with homemade pie pastry, I suggest you roll out the dough between two pieces of waxed paper. It makes the dough easier to handle and prevents sticking or using too much flour.

I like to use a pastry cloth and sleeve on my rolling pin, but you can use waxed paper or silicone mats. Experiment to discover what works best for you.

GRammy's apple Pie

There are many varieties of apples, and each has a slightly different flavor.
I like to combine two varieties in apple pie so that each bite tastes a little
different. My favorites are Golden Delicious and Haralson or Granny Smith.
McIntosh and Jonagold are also good cooking apples and widely available.
A traditional accompaniment (besides ice cream) for apple pie is a slice of
sharp Cheddar cheese.

MAKES 8 SERVINGS

> Pastry for 9-inch double-crust pie (see page 208)
> ¾ cup sugar
> 2 tablespoons all-purpose flour
> 1 teaspoon cinnamon
> 1 tablespoon orange juice
> 1 tablespoon grated orange peel
> 6 cups thinly sliced peeled apples (about 6 medium)
> ½ cup dried cranberries

Heat oven to 400°F with oven rack in lower third.

Roll out half of the pastry to an 11-inch circle. Loosely roll crust around rolling pin
and lift into 9-inch pie pan. Unroll and press along edges and bottom, making sure
pastry is not stretched.

Combine sugar, flour, cinnamon, orange juice, and orange peel in large bowl.
As you slice the apples, add them to bowl and toss until they are coated. Add
cranberries. Place filling in pastry shell.

Roll out remaining pastry to an 11-inch circle. Cut into ¾-inch strips. Lay 4 strips across filling in the same direction, using the longest strips for the center and shorter strips toward the edges. Weave together by lifting strips as crosswise strips are added. Press edges together and flute.

(For double-crust pie, do not cut top crust into strips. After placing over the fruit, press to seal the edges. Cut slits to allow steam to escape. Brush top with a little milk and sprinkle with cinnamon and sugar if desired.)

Bake 45 to 60 minutes or until crust is golden brown and juices are bubbly and thickened and apples are fork-tender. Cover edges with aluminum foil if crust is browning too much. Cool pie on wire cooling rack about 2 hours before cutting. Serve warm, at room temperature, or chilled.

BAKER'S NOTES: By placing the apples into the sugar mixture as they are sliced, the sugar and orange juice will keep them from browning.

If the crust edges become too brown, cut a 2-inch ring from a piece of aluminum foil and press it lightly over the edges.

SECRETS TO SUCCESS: It is easier for a beginning baker to weave the pastry for a topping rather than covering the whole pie with a top crust.

BLUEBERRY TART WITH VANILLA WHIPPED CREAM

I have been making this tart with the first blueberries of summer for over 20 years. If you're new to baking, you'll love this crust because it is made in the food processor and pressed, not rolled, into the tart pan. Lightly dust your fingers with flour if the pastry is sticky. I like to sift a little powdered sugar on top of the tart after it has cooled.

MAKES 8 SERVINGS

CRUST

1 cup all-purpose flour
2 tablespoons sugar
¼ teaspoon salt
½ cup butter, cut-up
1 tablespoon distilled white vinegar

FILLING

3 cups fresh blueberries, divided
¾ cup sugar
2 tablespoons all-purpose flour
1 teaspoon cinnamon

Vanilla Whipped Cream (see page 288)

Heat oven to 400°F with oven rack in middle.

CRUST

Combine flour, 2 tablespoons sugar, and salt in a food processor bowl. Add butter and pulse until dough resembles coarse crumbs with some pea-sized pieces. With processor running, add vinegar. Process until dough starts to clump together, about 10 seconds.

Gather dough into a ball and place in center of a 9-inch tart pan with removable bottom. Using your fingers, press dough out to the edges of the pan and up the sides. Lightly dust your fingers with a little flour if dough is sticky.

FILLING

Sprinkle 2 cups blueberries into the tart shell.

Combine sugar, flour, and cinnamon in small bowl and mix. Sprinkle evenly over the blueberries.

Bake 50 to 60 minutes or until filling is bubbling and sugar has dissolved. Remove tart from oven and press the reserved 1 cup of blueberries into the warm fruit. Cool on wire cooling rack at least 2 hours before cutting.

Chill Vanilla Whipped Cream until serving time, then mound over tart.

BAKER'S NOTES: The filling must be bubbling all over in order to dissolve the sugar.

SECRETS TO SUCCESS: The acid in the vinegar helps make the pastry tender. The vinegar flavor completely disappears during baking.

TURTLE CHEESECAKE PIE

Although this pie has pecans, chocolate, and caramel sauce, it is not over-whelmingly rich. The pecans in the crust are nicely toasted and add a pleasant little crunch. My favorite part of this recipe is that it can be made ahead and frozen until needed. Buy the best caramel sauce you can find because it adds the perfect silky finish.

MAKES 8 TO 10 SERVINGS

CRUST

¾ cup graham cracker crumbs

¾ cup finely chopped pecans

¼ cup sugar

⅓ cup butter, melted

FILLING

3 ounces unsweetened chocolate, chopped

2 tablespoons butter

½ of 8-ounce package cream cheese, softened

1 cup powdered sugar

1 teaspoon vanilla

1 cup whipping cream

Pecan halves

Caramel sauce

Heat oven to 375°F with oven rack in middle.

CRUST

Combine graham cracker crumbs, pecans, and sugar in medium bowl. Add melted butter and mix well. Spoon crust into 9-inch pie pan.

Using your fingers, press crumbs evenly into bottom and up sides of pie pan. Press along edge between bottom and side of pan so crust won't be too thick.

Bake 8 to 10 minutes until lightly browned and crust gives a little when touched lightly. Cool completely on wire cooling rack. This usually takes about 1 hour.

FILLING

Place chocolate and butter in a medium bowl set over, not in, simmering water until chocolate melts; or use a double boiler. Remove from heat. The last little lumps will melt as the mixture sits. Cool to room temperature. Reserve.

Beat cream cheese in bowl of a heavy-duty mixer on Medium speed until soft and creamy. Scrape down sides of bowl, and add powdered sugar and vanilla. Continue beating on High speed until smooth.

Gradually add whipping cream and continue beating until soft peaks form. Scrape down sides of bowl. Reduce mixer to Low speed and slowly beat in the melted chocolate. Continue beating until mixture stiffens slightly.

Spoon filling evenly into cooled crust. Smooth top and garnish with pecan halves. Chill several hours or freeze until serving. Spoon a little caramel sauce onto serving plates and top with pie.

BAKER'S NOTES: If the pie is frozen, remove it from the freezer and place it in refrigerator for several hours before serving. It can be cut and served while frozen, but I prefer to serve it with the filling softened.

SECRETS TO SUCCESS: Toast the pecan halves by placing in a 350°F oven for 8 to 10 minutes. Cool before placing on the pie.

CHOCOLATE PECAN PIE

We call this "birthday pie" at my house as it is my husband's favorite, and he requests it every year. Toasting the pecans really enhances their nutty flavor. Toast the pecans while you prepare the filling. The rum is optional—omit it if you prefer.

MAKES 8 SERVINGS

CRUST

Pastry for a 9-inch single-crust pie (see page 208)

FILLING

¾ cup sugar

1 cup light corn syrup

3 eggs, beaten

½ teaspoon salt

⅓ cup butter, melted

1 tablespoon dark rum, if desired

½ cup semisweet chocolate chips

1½ cup pecan halves, toasted

TOPPING

1 cup whipping cream

2 tablespoons powdered sugar

2 tablespoons dark rum, if desired

Heat oven to 375°F with oven rack in lower third.

CRUST

Roll out pastry into an 11-inch circle. Loosely roll dough around rolling pin and lift it into 9-inch pie pan. Unroll and press dough into pan edges and bottom, making sure that the pastry is not stretched.

FILLING

Combine sugar, corn syrup, eggs, and salt in medium bowl, and beat with a wire whisk until smooth. Slowly stir in butter and rum (if using) and mix well. Stir in chocolate chips and pecans and pour filling into prepared crust.

Bake 40 to 50 minutes or until filling is set except for 1-inch diameter section in center of pie. You can test this using a knife, which should come out clean but will be wet.

Cool on wire cooling rack about 2 hours before serving.

TOPPING

Beat whipping cream on High speed in bowl of a heavy-duty mixer fitted with the whisk until soft peaks form. Scrape down sides of bowl and add powdered sugar and rum (if using). Beat until sugar is dissolved and stiff peaks form. Chill until serving.

Place a dollop of whipped cream on each piece of pie before serving. When I serve this warm, I usually accompany it with ice cream.

BAKER'S NOTES: Toast the pecans at 350°F for 8 to 10 minutes. Watch them closely as they approach 8 minutes because they can burn quickly.

SECRETS TO SUCCESS: Whipping cream is easiest to beat when the cream, bowl, and whisk are cold. The chilled butter fat surrounds the air that is beaten in.

FRESH STRAWBERRY PIE

Strawberry Pie made with ripe red summer strawberries captures the heart of the season. The sauce, softly set, surrounds the berries with a little extra sweetness and highlights their fresh flavor. I select the prettiest berries to use whole for garnish.

SERVES 8

CRUST

Pastry for a 9-inch single-crust pie (see page 209), baked

FILLING

2 quarts strawberries

1 cup sugar

3 tablespoons cornstarch

1 tablespoon lemon juice

¼ cup water

½ teaspoon balsamic vinegar, if desired

Sweetened whipped cream

FILLING

Wash berries, remove stems, and slice. Place 2 cups sliced berries in medium bowl and crush using potato masher until juice is released. Reserve remaining sliced berries. Set aside several whole berries for garnish.

Mix sugar and cornstarch together in small bowl. Stir into the berries and let stand about 15 minutes to draw out more juice. Place crushed berries, water, lemon juice, and vinegar in medium saucepan. Cook over medium heat about 5 minutes, stirring constantly, until mixture comes to a boil and is thick and clear. Reduce heat and continue cooking 1 minute longer, stirring constantly. Cool to room temperature, stirring occasionally.

Place remaining sliced berries in baked shell. Pour the sauce over them and stir a little. Refrigerate pie until sauce sets. Serve with whipped cream (see page 10). Garnish with fresh strawberries.

> BAKER'S NOTES: If you don't have a potato masher, crush the berries with a fork or pastry blender.
>
> The thickened juices splatter and are very hot, so I use a spoon with a long handle for stirring. Cooking after the filling becomes clear is needed for a firm filling.
>
> SECRETS TO SUCCESS: If you don't want to take the time to make a crust from scratch, you can purchase a frozen pie pastry that is ready to bake. Just follow the directions on the package.

DUTCH aPPLe PIe

The "Dutch" in the title refers to the Pennsylvania Dutch in eastern Pennsylvania, as far as I know. This pie can be in the oven in no time flat if you purchase the crust and add fruit and the recipe's sweet, crumbly topping. Use apples that are good for cooking such as Jonathan or Golden Delicious.

SERVES 8

CRUST

Pastry for a 9-inch single-crust pie (see page 208)

FILLING

¾ cup sugar

1 tablespoon all-purpose flour

1 teaspoon cinnamon

6 cups thinly sliced peeled apples (6 to 8 medium)

1 tablespoon lemon juice

TOPPING

       ⅓ cup sugar

       ⅓ cup all-purpose flour

       3 tablespoons cold butter

Heat oven to 375°F with oven rack in lower third.

CRUST

Roll out pastry into an 11-inch circle. Loosely roll dough around rolling pin and lift it into 9-inch pie pan. Unroll and press dough into pan edges and bottom, making sure that the pastry is not stretched.

FILLING

Combine sugar, flour, and cinnamon in large bowl. As you slice the apples, add them to the bowl. Sprinkle them with lemon juice and toss.

Spoon apple mixture evenly into prepared crust.

TOPPING

Combine sugar and flour in medium bowl. Cut in butter with pastry blender until mixture resembles coarse crumbs with some pea-sized pieces. Sprinkle evenly over the apples.

Bake 40 to 55 minutes or until apples are fork-tender and juices thickened. Cover loosely with aluminum foil if pie becomes very dark. Cool on wire cooling rack at least 2 hours before serving. Serve slightly warm.

BAKER'S NOTE: I have also made this pie with peaches and nectarines. Because these fruits are juicier than apples, increase the flour in the filling to 2 tablespoons.

PUMPKIN STREUSEL PIE

Contribute a pumpkin pie for Thanksgiving dinner, and you will be a very popular guest. Every hostess always appreciates a pie, as it's one less thing to be done. The filling is the traditional standard, but the crunchy pecan topping adds a spicy nuttiness. The most important step in this recipe is not to overbake the pie.

SERVES 8

CRUST

Pastry for a 9-inch single-crust pie (see page 208)

FILLING

1 (15-ounce) can pumpkin
¾ cup firmly packed brown sugar
2 eggs, slightly beaten
1 teaspoon cinnamon
¼ teaspoon salt
1 (12-ounce) can evaporated milk

TOPPING

¼ cup firmly packed brown sugar
¼ cup all-purpose flour
3 tablespoons cold butter
½ cup chopped pecans, toasted

Sweetened Whipped Cream (see page 10)

Heat oven to 425°F with oven rack in lower third.

CRUST

Roll out pastry into an 11-inch circle. Loosely roll dough around rolling pin and lift it into 9-inch pie pan. Unroll and press dough into pan edges and bottom, making sure that the pastry is not stretched.

FILLING

Combine pumpkin and ¾ cup brown sugar in large bowl and mix until sugar dissolves and no lumps remain. Add eggs, cinnamon, and salt and whisk until smooth. Stir in milk. Pour pumpkin mixture into pastry shell.

Bake 15 minutes.

TOPPING

Combine ¼ cup brown sugar with flour. Cut in butter with pastry blender until mixture resembles coarse crumbs with some pea-sized pieces. Stir in pecans.

Reduce oven to 350°F. Crumble topping around outer edge of pie. Bake an additional 30 to 40 minutes or until set in center and a knife comes out clean although it will be wet. Cool on wire cooling rack at least 4 hours before serving. Serve with whipped cream. Store in the refrigerator.

BAKER'S NOTES: Test for doneness about ½ inch away from pie's center—the filling should look set and not jiggle. When pumpkin pie is baked too long, the crust will become soggy.

Toast the pecans at 350°F. Place the nuts on a baking sheet and bake 8 to 10 minutes. Watch them because they burn quickly.

COUNTRY-STYLE PEACH PIE

Summery fresh peaches full of luscious juice are the reason this pie is a winner. I've placed the crust in a deep-dish pie plate so the center can be heaped with peaches, and then the dough can be folded over the filling. This pie needs nothing else—the peaches are wonderful.

SERVES 8

CRUST

Pastry for a single-crust 9-inch pie (see page 208)

FILLING

½ cup firmly packed brown sugar
3 tablespoons cornstarch
1 teaspoon cinnamon
¼ teaspoon freshly grated nutmeg
6 cups sliced peeled fresh peaches (about 8 medium)
1 tablespoon lemon juice

TOPPING

⅓ cup all-purpose flour
¼ cup sugar
3 tablespoons butter

Heat oven to 400°F with oven rack in lower third.

CRUST

Roll out pastry to a 12-inch circle. Loosely roll dough around the rolling pin and lift it into a 9-inch deep-dish pie plate. Unroll and press dough along bottom, making sure that the pastry is not stretched. Dough will overlap pie plate edges.

FILLING

Combine brown sugar, cornstarch, cinnamon, and nutmeg in large bowl. Slice peaches into the bowl and sprinkle with lemon juice. Toss gently and spoon into the pie shell.

Fold overlapping edges of pastry toward the center and over the fruit. There will be about 2 inches of fruit in center left uncovered.

TOPPING

Mix flour and sugar in small bowl. Cut in butter with pastry blender until mixture resembles coarse crumbs with some pea-sized pieces. Sprinkle over the fruit in center of pie.

Bake 50 to 60 minutes or until crust is browned and bubbling juices are thickened. Cool at least 2 hours before serving.

BAKER'S NOTES: If you don't have a deep-dish pie plate, reduce the peaches to 5 cups and use a 9-inch pie pan.

Drop the peaches into boiling water for 20 seconds and then place them in cold water. This makes them easy to peel.

SECRETS TO SUCCESS: I like the flavor of the freshly grated nutmeg because it is more delicate than ground. If you don't have fresh nutmeg, just omit it.

CRAB AND ASPARAGUS QUICHE

When asparagus first appears in the spring, I serve it roasted to capture its fresh flavor. As the season progresses, I have lots of additional ways of serving it, such as in quiche, which is appropriate for any meal of the day. Select asparagus stalks that are slim, bright green and crisp, with tight buds at the tips. Arrange the spears in a spokes design for a fancy presentation.

SERVES 8

CRUST

Pastry for a 9-inch single-crust pie (see page 208)

FILLING

8 fresh asparagus spears

6 ounces (about 1 cup) crabmeat

1 cup shredded fontina cheese

1 cup whole milk

4 eggs, beaten

1 teaspoon grated lemon peel

½ teaspoon dry mustard

½ teaspoon coarse salt

Heat oven to 400°F with oven rack in middle.

CRUST

Roll out pastry into an 11-inch circle. Loosely roll dough around rolling pin and lift it into pie pan. Unroll and press dough into pan edges and bottom, making sure that the pastry is not stretched. Flute edges if desired.

Bake crust 10 to 15 minutes or until it begins to brown.

FILLING

Place asparagus spears in flat dish with 2 tablespoons water and microwave on High 2 minutes to partially cook. Drain well. Asparagus can also be blanched in boiling water.

Sprinkle crabmeat into bottom of partially baked pastry shell and top with cheese. Arrange asparagus spears in a spokes fashion over the cheese.

Combine milk, eggs, lemon peel, mustard, and salt in medium bowl and whisk until mixed. Carefully pour the custard into the crust.

Bake 25 to 35 minutes or until custard is set and a knife inserted in center comes out clean although it will be wet. Cool 10 minutes before serving to allow custard to set up.

Serve warm, at room temperature, or chilled. Store any remaining quiche in the refrigerator.

BAKER'S NOTES: Fontina cheese is a creamy Italian cheese with a nutty flavor made from cow's milk. Swiss cheese can be used as a substitute.

SECRETS TO SUCCESS: Before cooking fresh asparagus, snap off the tough bottoms of the stalks and rinse thoroughly to remove any dirt. If you break the asparagus into 2-inch pieces, you will get some in every bite.

GRAHAM CRACKER VANILLA CREAM PIE

What can be more comforting than creamy vanilla pudding and graham crackers? The filling is a basic cornstarch pudding that is enriched with egg yolks. It is essential to warm the yolks with some of the pudding before adding them to the hot mixture; otherwise they will set immediately. When beating the meringue, beat until the egg whites form stiff, glossy peaks when you lift the beaters. Remember to seal the edges of the crust.

SERVES 8

CRUST

1 ½ cups graham cracker crumbs
¼ cup sugar
¼ cup butter, melted

FILLING

¾ cup sugar
¼ cup cornstarch
⅛ teaspoon salt
3 cups milk
3 egg yolks, beaten
2 tablespoons butter
1 ½ teaspoons vanilla

MERINGUE

3 egg whites
½ teaspoon cream of tartar
6 tablespoons sugar

Heat oven to 350°F with oven rack in middle.

CRUST

Combine crumbs, sugar, and melted butter in medium bowl. Press crust into a 9-inch pie plate. Bake 8 to 10 minutes or until crust is lightly browned. Cool on wire cooling rack.

FILLING

Place sugar, cornstarch, and salt in medium saucepan. Slowly add milk, stirring until cornstarch dissolves. Cook over medium heat, stirring constantly, until mixture comes to a boil. Stir the pudding so it doesn't stick to the bottom or sides of pan. Reduce heat to low, and boil for 1 minute, stirring constantly.

Remove pan from heat. Slowly pour about ¾ cup of the hot pudding into the yolks while whisking constantly. Whisk yolk mixture into the hot pudding.

Return pan to the heat and cook on low, stirring constantly, about 1 minute or until mixture thickens. Remove from heat and stir in butter and vanilla.

Pour filling into crust and cover surface with plastic wrap to prevent skin from forming.

meringue

Beat egg whites and cream of tartar on high speed in bowl of a heavy-duty mixer fitted with the whisk until soft peaks form. Gradually add sugar, 1 tablespoon at a time. Continue beating until glossy and stiff peaks form. When you lift beaters, the meringue should rise and peaks remain upright. Be sure to beat until the sugar is dissolved.

Remove plastic wrap from the pie and spread meringue over the warm filling. Spread it to the edges and seal it to the crust. Sprinkle about 1 teaspoon graham cracker crumbs over the top.

Bake about 10 minutes or until lightly browned. Cool on wire cooling rack to room temperature. Refrigerate at least 4 hours before serving.

> BAKER'S NOTES: Follow the directions for the custard filling carefully and cook on low after adding the yolks. Warming the eggs before adding them to the milk mixture is called "tempering."
>
> Do not let the pudding boil or the eggs will curdle.
>
> I use a heavy saucepan for the filling so that the bottom of the pan won't become too hot. Always use medium to low heat for eggs.

banana cream pie

I recommend using bananas that are only just ripe for this pie because very ripe bananas will turn brown in the pudding. Homemade vanilla pudding has a velvety feel and understated flavor that is hard to match, but it takes extra time. For a very quick dessert, bake the crust and buy a box of vanilla pudding for the filling. Serve with a squirt of whipped cream from an aerosol can.

SERVES 8

CRUST

  1 ½ cups graham cracker crumbs
  ¼ cup sugar
  ¼ cup butter, melted

FILLING

¾ cup sugar
¼ cup cornstarch
⅛ teaspoon salt
3 cups milk
3 egg yolks, beaten
2 tablespoons butter
1 teaspoon vanilla
1 sliced ripe banana

Vanilla Whipped Cream (see page 288)

Heat oven to 350°F with oven rack in middle.

CRUST

Combine crumbs, sugar, and melted butter in medium bowl. Press crust into a 9-inch pie plate. Bake 8 to 10 minutes or until crust is lightly browned. Cool on wire cooling rack.

FILLING

Place sugar, cornstarch, and salt in medium saucepan. Slowly add milk, stirring until cornstarch dissolves. Cook over medium heat, stirring constantly, until mixture comes to a boil. Stir pudding so it doesn't stick to bottom or sides of pan. Reduce heat to low, and boil for 1 minute, stirring constantly.

Remove pan from heat. Slowly pour about ¾ cup of hot pudding into the egg yolks while whisking constantly. Whisk yolk mixture into the hot pudding. Return pan to the heat, and cook on low, stirring constantly, about 1 minute or until mixture thickens. Remove from heat and stir in butter and vanilla.

Pour half of the filling into the crust and cover with banana slices. Add remaining filling and cover surface with plastic wrap to prevent skin from forming.

Chill at least 4 hours before serving. Spread whipped cream over top before serving.

BAKER'S NOTES: Because bananas turn brown after they are sliced, this pie is best the day it is baked, but it can be refrigerated for 2 to 3 days.

Egg whites can be frozen for later use. Place them in a freezer container and freeze.

SECRETS TO SUCCESS: Baking the graham cracker crust is important because it turns the crumbs into a crust. Don't be tempted to skip the baking.

A heat-resistant spatula makes it easy to stir the hot pudding during cooking.

Lemon meringue pie

Lemons are always associated with the freshness of spring even though they are available year round. The grated lemon peel adds a strong citrus note to the tangy tartness in the filling. Try this after you have some experience with baking because it takes more time than most of the recipes in the book—but the flavor payoff is definitely worth the work.

SERVES 8

CRUST

Pastry for a 9-inch single-crust pie (see page 209), baked

FILLING

1 ¼ cups sugar

⅓ cup cornstarch

2 tablespoons all-purpose flour

¼ teaspoon salt

1 ½ cups water

3 egg yolks, beaten

2 tablespoons butter

½ cup freshly squeezed lemon juice

1 tablespoon grated lemon peel

MERINGUE

3 egg whites, room temperature

¼ teaspoon cream of tartar

6 tablespoons sugar

FILLING

Place sugar, cornstarch, flour and salt in medium saucepan. Slowly add water, stirring until cornstarch dissolves. Cook over medium heat, stirring constantly, until mixture comes to a boil. Stir pudding so it doesn't stick to the bottom or sides of the pan. Reduce heat to low and boil for 1 minute, stirring constantly. Mixture will be clear and very thick.

Remove pan from heat. Slowly pour about ¾ cup of hot pudding into the egg yolks while whisking constantly. Whisk the yolk mixture into the hot pudding. Return pan to the heat and cook on low, stirring constantly, about 1 minute or until mixture thickens.

Remove from heat and stir in butter, lemon juice, and lemon peel. Pour into crust and cover surface with a piece of plastic wrap to prevent skin from forming.

Heat oven to 350°F with oven rack in middle.

meringue

Beat egg whites and cream of tartar on high speed in bowl of a heavy-duty mixer fitted with the whisk until soft peaks form. Gradually add sugar, one tablespoon at a time. Continue beating until glossy and stiff peaks form. When you lift the beaters, meringue should form peaks that remain upright. Be sure to beat until sugar is dissolved.

Remove plastic wrap from pie and spread meringue over the warm filling and seal it to the crust. Bake about 10 minutes or until meringue is lightly browned. Cool on cooling rack. Chill at least 4 hours before serving.

BAKER'S NOTES: You will need 2 to 3 lemons for ½ cup lemon juice. Roll the lemons under your palm, back and forth on the counter before squeezing and the lemons will yield more juice.

A microplane grater is a kitchen essential and makes it very easy to grate the peel without grating the pithy white layer. Grate the peel before cutting and squeezing juice.

I use a long-handled spoon or heatproof spatula for stirring so that I am not spattered with the filling as it boils.

SECRET TO SUCCESS: It is better for the appearance of a meringue pie if it's not baked on a humid day. The meringue pulls the moisture from the air and it appears as drops on the baked meringue. The pie will still taste delicious!

Lemon mascarpone Tarts

Mascarpone cheese is a rich, silky Italian triple-cream cheese. It has become widely known and readily available because it is used in the ubiquitous Tiramisu. Purchase lemon curd to simplify the preparation of these beautiful tarts. You can use any colorful combination of fresh fruit for toppings: strawberries, raspberries, and kiwi fruit sparkle with color.

MAKES 8 TARTS

CRUST

1 ½ cups all-purpose flour

2 tablespoons sugar

½ teaspoon salt

½ cup cold butter, cut-up

3 tablespoons ice water

FILLING

8 ounces mascarpone cheese

1 cup whipping cream

2 tablespoons powdered sugar

⅓ cup lemon curd, room temperature (see page 290)

Fresh fruit

Heat oven to 425°F with oven rack in middle.

CRUST

Place flour, sugar, and salt in food processor bowl. Pulse about 5 times to mix. Add butter. Process until coarse crumbs form with some pea-sized pieces. Add 3 tablespoons ice water and process until dough begins to clump together. Process about

10 seconds. If large clumps do not form, add a little more water, 1 teaspoon at a time. Place dough on well-floured work surface and gather it together.

Divide dough into 8 pieces. Press each into bottoms of 8 (3-inch) tart pans. Press firmly against sides of pans. Pierce crusts generously with a fork.

Place tart shells on a baking sheet. Bake 12 minutes or until crusts are nicely browned. Cool to room temperature before filling. Gently release shells from the pans.

FILLING

Beat mascarpone cheese and whipping cream on low speed in bowl of a heavy-duty mixer fitted with the whisk until mixture begins to thicken. Scrape down sides of bowl. Increase mixer to high speed and beat until soft peaks form. Reduce mixer speed to medium.

Add powdered sugar and beat until mixed. By hand, stir in lemon curd. There can still be some streaks remaining. Divide the lemon cream into the tart shells.

Garnish with fresh fruit and refrigerate. Tarts can be made 4 hours ahead.

BAKER'S NOTE: If the lemon curd is cold, it will stiffen the cream immediately. Don't over mix or the mascarpone will curdle.

caramel macadamia Tarts

Once I purchased small tart pans, I was surprised at how often I used them. I recommend the pans with removable bottoms simply because this makes it easier to remove the tartlets. Press the dough up the sides of the pans so the filling won't stick to the sides. Macadamia nuts are native to Australia, but the largest exporter of the nuts today is Hawaii.

MAKES 6 TARTS

CRUST

1 cup all-purpose flour

3 tablespoons unsweetened cocoa powder

¼ cup powdered sugar

⅛ teaspoon salt

⅓ cup butter

1 egg yolk

1 teaspoon vanilla

3 teaspoons milk, if needed

FILLING

½ cup firmly packed brown sugar

1 tablespoon flour

⅔ cup whipping cream

½ cup chopped macadamia nuts

CRUST

Place flour, cocoa, powdered sugar, and salt into a food processor bowl. Pulse 5 times to mix. Add butter and process until mixture resembles coarse crumbs with some pea-sized pieces. Add egg yolk and vanilla and pulse until dough begins to form clumps. If clumps do not form, add milk, 1 teaspoon at a time, and process until dough forms.

Gather dough together and shape into a ball. Wrap in plastic wrap and refrigerate 1 hour or until chilled.

Heat oven to 400°F with oven rack in middle.

Place dough on a lightly floured surface and divide into 6 pieces. Press into bottoms of 6 (3-inch) tart pans. Press dough firmly against sides of pans. Extend dough a little above pan sides to prevent filling from sticking.

Place tart shells on a cookie sheet and bake 8 to 10 minutes. Reduce oven to 375°F.

FILLING

Combine brown sugar, flour, and whipping cream in small bowl. Divide filling into the tart shells. Add about 2 tablespoons chopped macadamias to each tart.

Bake tarts 20 to 25 minutes or until filling is bubbling. Place tarts on cooling rack and cool to room temperature. Carefully remove tarts from pans.

BAKER'S NOTES: Do not pierce the tart crust with a fork before baking because the filling will leak.

I measure the whipping cream into a 4-cup glass measuring cup and then add the brown sugar and flour. The cup is large enough to mix the ingredients and makes it easy to pour the filling into the shells.

SECRETS TO SUCCESS: The nuts won't be covered with filling if they're added after the filling is in the tart shells.

WILD MUSHROOM TARTLETS

Wild mushrooms add a woodsy flavor to these elegant tarts. I usually use an assortment of shiitake, chanterelle, and baby bellas, depending on what's available. White cremini mushrooms work well but don't have as much flavor. Dried porcini mushrooms are expensive, but one or two really make a difference.

MAKES 6 TARTS

CRUST

    1 cup all-purpose flour
¼ cup butter, cut-up
1 (3-ounce) package cream cheese, cut up

FILLING

    1 tablespoon butter
1 tablespoon olive oil
1 shallot, chopped
8 ounces fresh wild mushrooms, sliced
2 dried porcini mushrooms, soaked in hot water, chopped
½ teaspoon salt
1 teaspoon chopped fresh thyme, or ¼ teaspoon dried thyme leaves
1 tablespoon Madeira or brandy
⅓ cup whipping cream
¼ cup sour cream
1 egg yolk

Heat oven to 400°F with oven rack in middle.

CRUST

Place flour in food processor bowl. Add butter and cream cheese and pulse until dough forms.

Divide dough into 6 pieces and press into bottoms of 6 (3-inch) tart pans. Press firmly against sides of pans. If dough extends a little above pan sides, it will prevent filling from sticking.

Bake 10 minutes or until edges are lightly browned. Reduce oven to 350°F.

FILLING

Heat butter and olive oil in 9-inch skillet and add shallot. Cook over medium heat, stirring occasionally, until tender. Add fresh mushrooms and increase heat to medium-high. Cook, stirring constantly, until mushrooms are cooked and liquid evaporated. Add the porcini. Stir in salt, thyme, and Madeira and scrape to loosen any browned bits from bottom of pan. Remove from heat and cool to lukewarm.

Combine whipping cream, sour cream, and egg yolk in small bowl and mix well. Spoon into tart shells, using about 1 ½ to 2 tablespoons per shell. Top with 2 tablespoons mushrooms mixture. Place tarts on a cookie sheet.

Bake 20 to 25 minutes or until filling is set. Cool 5 minutes on wire cooling rack and remove from pans. Serve warm or at room temperature.

BAKER'S NOTES: Dried porcini mushrooms must be soaked in very hot water before using. Cover the mushrooms with hot water and let stand 20 minutes. Drain and chop.

Remove the stems from the shiitake mushrooms because they won't soften when they are cooked.

SECRET TO SUCCESS: You can use a jellyroll pan with sides to hold the tarts while baking. This prevents the pans from sidling off.

Use a mushroom brush or a towel to brush dirt from the mushrooms. Don't rinse because the mushrooms will absorb too much water.

CRANBERRY WALNUT TARTLETS

Be sure to try this with crème fraiche—the puckery cranberry filling of the tarts contrasts delightfully with the silky crème. Although cranberries appear fresh in the markets in the fall, they are also available frozen year round, so you can bake these crimson delights any time.

MAKES 8 TARTS

CRUST

1 ½ cups all-purpose flour
2 tablespoons sugar
½ teaspoon salt
½ cup cold butter, cut-up
3–4 tablespoons ice water

FILLING

1 cup firmly packed brown sugar
2 tablespoons flour
⅓ cup light corn syrup
1 ½ teaspoons vanilla
2 eggs, beaten
2 tablespoons butter, melted
¾ cup chopped walnuts
¾ cup chopped fresh or frozen, cranberries
½–¾ cup crème fraîche (see page 290)

Heat oven to 350°F with oven rack in lower third.

CRUST

Place flour, sugar, and salt in food processor bowl. Pulse about 5 times to mix. Add butter. Process until coarse crumbs form with some pea-sized pieces. Add 3 tablespoons ice water and process until dough begins to clump together. Process about 10 seconds. If large clumps do not form, add a little more water, 1 teaspoon at a time. Place dough on well-floured work surface, and gather it together into a ball.

Divide dough into 8 equal pieces. Press into bottoms of 8 (3-inch) tart pans. Press firmly against sides of pans. Extend the dough a little above the sides to prevent filling from sticking.

FILLING

Combine brown sugar and flour in medium bowl. Add corn syrup, vanilla, and eggs. Whisk until mixture is smooth. No lumps of brown sugar or flour should remain.

Stir in butter, walnuts, and cranberries. Divide filling into prepared shells, using about ¼ cup for each. Gently even out surfaces of the tarts so that nuts and cranberries are evenly spaced.

Bake 28 to 33 minutes or until knife inserted in center comes out clean. Crusts should be golden brown. Cool tarts on wire cooling rack. Remove from pans. Serve warm or at room temperature with crème fraîche.

> BAKER'S NOTES: Place tarts on a jellyroll pan or cookie sheet lined with parchment paper in case filling runs over the sides.
>
> Most supermarkets carry crème fraîche, but you can also make your own with buttermilk and whipping cream (see page 290).

TOURTIÈRE

Tourtière is a French Canadian meat pie with a lightly spiced pork filling that is traditionally served on Christmas Eve. Serve it warm from the oven, or make it ahead and serve it at room temperature or reheated. You might wish to use refrigerated pastry as a time-saver during the busy holiday season.

SERVES 8

CRUST

Pastry for a 9-inch double-crust pie (see page 208)

FILLING

1 tablespoon olive oil
1 cup chopped onion (1 medium)
1 teaspoon minced garlic
1½ pounds ground pork
2 tablespoons all-purpose flour
½ teaspoon cinnamon
½ teaspoon poultry seasoning
¼ teaspoon salt
⅛ teaspoon ground mace
1 cup chicken broth
Fresh ground pepper
2 tablespoons chopped fresh parsley

CRUST

Roll out half of pastry into an 11-inch circle. Loosely roll dough around rolling pin and lift it into pie pan. Unroll and press dough into pan edges and bottom, making sure that the pastry is not stretched. Chill while preparing filling.

FILLING

Heat olive oil in 9-inch skillet over medium heat. Add onion and cook until it softens, stirring occasionally. Add garlic and cook 30 seconds.

Crumble pork into the pan. Cook over medium-high heat until meat is well browned and all pink has disappeared. Drain off fat. Reduce heat to low. Stir flour into meat and sprinkle with seasonings. Add broth and stir until sauce thickens. Season with pepper and add parsley. Remove from heat and cool to lukewarm.

Heat oven to 400°F with oven rack in lower third.

Spoon lukewarm filling into the pastry. Roll remaining dough into 11-inch circle and place over filling. Pinch edges to seal. Flute the edges if desired. Cut several slits for steam to escape during baking.

Bake 30 to 40 minutes or until golden brown. Serve warm or at room temperature. Store pie in refrigerator.

BAKER'S NOTE: You can reheat the pie in about 30 minutes in a 350°F oven.

SECRETS TO SUCCESS: During the busy holiday season, I sometime purchase the pie crusts because it's so convenient.

seafood potpie

A creamy rich sauce surrounds tender seafood with the fresh flavors of lemon and dill in this updated comfort food. I have also prepared this with refrigerated, pasteurized crabmeat as well as high-quality canned crab from the fish counter in my supermarket. Purchase peeled and deveined shrimp and delicate bay scallops.

MAKES 4 POTPIES

CRUST

Pastry for a 9-inch single-crust pie (see page 208)

FILLING

3 tablespoons butter, divided

8 ounces small whole mushrooms

½ pound peeled, deveined small shrimp (26 to 30 per pound)

¼ pound bay scallops, rinsed

¼ cup white wine

1 (6-ounce) package or can claw crabmeat

sauce

3 tablespoons butter

¼ cup all-purpose flour

1 cup half-and-half

¼ cup chopped green onions

2 teaspoons chopped fresh dill

1 teaspoon lemon juice

Salt and pepper, to taste

Hot pepper sauce, if desired

1 egg

1 teaspoon water

CRUST

Roll out pastry into a 12-inch circle. Cut 5- to 6-inch circles to fit 4 small, oven-proof soup bowls or small pie plates.

FILLING

Melt 1 tablespoon butter in medium skillet. Add mushrooms and cook on medium-high until tender. Add a little more butter, if necessary. Remove mushrooms and set aside.

Add remaining 2 tablespoons butter and shrimp and cook 2 minutes. Add scallops and continue cooking until shrimp are bright pink and scallops are opaque. Add wine and simmer briefly until it evaporates. Remove from heat. Stir in crabmeat and mushrooms.

Melt butter over medium heat in small saucepan. Stir in flour and cook 1 minute, stirring constantly. Add half-and-half and cook until thickened, stirring constantly.

Remove from heat. Stir in seafood filling and green onions, dill, and lemon juice. Season to taste with salt and pepper. Season with hot pepper sauce, if desired.

Beat egg with water in small bowl.

Heat oven to 425°F with oven rack in lower third.

Spoon about ¾ cup of seafood filling into each oven-proof bowl. Brush the egg wash on rims of bowls. Place pastry over each bowl and press to seal it to the edge. Cut a few slits to allow steam to escape. Brush pastry tops lightly with egg wash.

Bake 15 to 18 minutes or until crust is golden brown. Allow potpies to cool a few minutes before serving.

BAKER'S NOTE: The sauce for the seafood is a basic, but rich, white sauce. I have the best luck by adding the liquid all at once and beating with a whisk until the sauce thickens.

SECRETS TO SUCCESS: I like to press a dill frond on top of the crust before baking.

---

chapter eleven

yeast breads and ROLLS

HOMEMADE BREAD IS ALL ABOUT comfort. It takes several hours to make yeast breads, but while the dough is rising or baking, you can do other things. Every so often the dough needs to be punched down or shaped, but once the dough is made, there isn't much else to do but be patient.

Two of the most important steps in making bread depend on temperature. The yeast must be softened in warm water, and temperature is the best way to measure doneness in a large loaf. An instant-read thermometer accurately measures both.

Yeast breads and rolls follow the same basic steps: soften the yeast, mix the dough, knead the dough, provide a warm place for rising, shape into loaves or rolls, rise again, and bake.

DISSOLVING THE YEAST

Yeast requires liquid, food (sugar and flour), and warmth to grow. Dissolving the yeast in warm water is called "proofing" because you are actually proving that the yeast is alive. The yeast can also be combined with the flour and the warm water added to both; using this method, the water can be warmer, and the dough will start rising a little faster. Always use yeast before the expiration date on the package.

MIXING AND KNEADING THE DOUGH

Follow directions in the recipe for mixing the dough. Once the dough is mixed, it must be kneaded. Kneading develops the elastic gluten strands from the flour proteins, giving structure to the bread. Always save some flour to add during kneading. Because flour can absorb water from the air, the amount needed for the dough varies. As the dough is kneaded, it becomes less sticky and requires less flour.

Too much flour will make your bread and rolls dry. It is better to have a slightly sticky dough than one that is too dry.

The tenderness of sweet yeast bread is a result of the sugar and fat interfering with the gluten formation, and sometimes these doughs require more kneading.

Today, most of us have a heavy-duty mixer with a dough hook attachment. I think this is an easy way to knead dough, but I always finish kneading the bread by hand. To me, making bread is about touch—pushing the dough away with the palms of your hands and feeling the strength and elasticity of the dough.

RISING and SHaPING

After kneading, the dough needs to rise in a warm place until doubled. Place it in an oiled bowl, turning to coat with oil. Cover and let rise. Next, punch down and shape. Then let it rise again and bake. The amount of time required for rising is dependent on warmth. Dough has risen enough for the first rise when it has doubled in size and won't spring back when you poke your finger into it.

An easy way to make a warm place for dough is to place a wire rack over a 13 x 9-inch pan of hot water. The top of a warm range or a turned-off oven are other possibilities.

After rising, punch the dough down to deflate it by pressing out excess air. Shape the dough as directed in the recipe and place on or in the greased pan to be used for baking. If you have any trouble shaping the dough, allow it to rest 5 to 10 minutes so that the gluten relaxes; then it will be easy to shape. After the second rise, the dough is ready if a gentle touch leaves only a slight imprint.

BaKING THE BReaD

I can't think of anything that smells better than baking bread, unless it's scent of warm caramel rolls. A test for doneness relies on the sound made when the loaf is tapped. It should sound hollow. But I find the best test, once again, is to insert an instant-read thermometer. The interior of the bread should be 190°F or a little higher. Although it is very hard not to slice and taste your bread immediately, it must cool slightly or it will collapse as it's sliced.

The best way to serve any yeast bread is warm from the oven. However, it's nice to have some for later. Most bread keeps 1 to 2 days at room temperature, but breads with honey and butter keep a little longer. After the loaf is completely cool, wrap it tightly and store at room temperature. For longer storage, wrap it tightly and freeze up to 3 months. Thaw at room temperature and reheat. Wrap bread in aluminum foil and reheat it at 350°F for 15 to 30 minutes. Unwrap the bread during the last 5 minutes for a crisper crust.

INGREDIENTS

Bread flour is easily found today in the baking sections of most supermarkets because bread machines have increased the demand for it. Bread flour is higher in protein—and thus gluten—than other flours. Because of the high amount of protein, it requires longer kneading than doughs made with all-purpose flour. Many bakers, however, only use all-purpose flour.

Whole-wheat flour doesn't have as much gluten as white flour and should always be combined with bread flour or all-purpose flour when it is used in breads. If used alone, whole-wheat bread is heavy and dense. To maintain freshness longer, store whole-wheat flour in your freezer.

My recipes use active-dry and fast-rising yeast. Be sure to check the expiration date on the package. Use a thermometer to measure the water temperature accurately (see How to Dissolve Yeast, page 11).

It is important to use the correct amount of salt because it conditions the dough and controls the growth of the yeast. Add it with the flour, as it kills the yeast when added to the yeast mixture alone

Sugar, butter, and eggs enrich the dough and make sweet, tender rolls and breads. Margarine can be substituted for butter in breads if cholesterol is an issue. It performs exactly the same as butter, but the butter flavor is lost. Brown sugar and honey help hold moisture in the bread so it will keep a little longer.

EQUIPMENT

A heavy-duty mixer with a dough hook makes it easy to prepare yeast doughs. Large bowls, basic baking pans such as 9 x 5-inch loaf pans, 13 x 9-inch pans for rolls, cookie sheets, standard muffin pans, and pizza pans are used most often in bread baking. Don't forget an instant-read thermometer and a serrated knife for slicing.

BasIC WHITe BreaD

The yeasty aroma of homemade bread promises the warmth and comfort of home. Heavy-duty mixers with dough hooks for kneading have made home-made bread a lot less work. After kneading with the mixer, I always knead a little by hand because making bread is a tactile experience for me. At this point most of the work has been done, and now it's a matter of patience. But you'll agree that it's worth it when you take your first bite.

MAKES 2 LOAVES

> 1 cup milk
> 1 cup water
> 2 tablespoons sugar
> 1 (¼-ounce) package active dry yeast
> ¼ cup solid vegetable shortening
> 2 teaspoons salt
> 5–6 cups bread flour, divided

Heat milk, water, and sugar in a small saucepan over medium heat to 105 to 115°F. Remove pan from heat and sprinkle yeast over the liquid. Add shortening and let mixture stand 5 minutes. The shortening doesn't have to melt.

Place the salt and 2½ cups of flour in bowl of a heavy-duty mixer. Add yeast mixture and beat on Medium speed for 3 minutes. By hand, stir in about 2½ cups more flour or enough to make a soft dough.

If kneading with a heavy-duty mixer, follow manufacturer's directions.

To knead by hand, place the dough on a well-floured surface and shape it roughly into a ball. Place your fingers on top, curled slightly over the ball, and pull the dough toward you. Then push dough away, using the palms of your hands. Turn dough ¼ turn and repeat.

When you begin kneading, the dough will be sticky. Add flour a little at a time. As you knead, keep your fingers together and use the palms of your hands. Knead dough 8 to 10 minutes until it is smooth and elastic. You should not use more than 6 cups of flour, total.

To judge whether the dough has been sufficiently kneaded, place dough on work surface, pull both ends gently, and release. The dough should be elastic and spring back. The dough should also be smooth and have little blisters of air that you can see under the surface.

Shape dough into a ball by pulling sides underneath to form a smooth top. Place it, top side down, in an oiled bowl. Turn the dough right side up, thus coating it with a little oil. Cover loosely with plastic wrap.

Let dough rise in a warm place until it doubles in size, about 1 hour. When it has doubled, the imprint will remain when you poke two fingers into the dough.

Grease bottom and part way up sides of two 9 x 5-inch loaf pans.

Punch dough down, and place it on a lightly floured surface. Cut dough in half.

Roll out one of the halves to a 14 x 8-inch rectangle. If dough becomes difficult to shape, cover and let stand 5 to 10 minutes to relax the gluten. Roll dough up from the short side, and pinch edges to seal. Place in a greased pan, seam side down. Repeat with other portion of dough. Loosely cover loaf pans with plastic wrap.

Let dough rise again until doubled, about 30 minutes. Test by pressing dough lightly. If your finger leaves only a slight imprint the dough is ready. It usually takes about half the time for the second rise as for the first.

Heat oven to 375°F with oven rack in lower third. Bake loaves 35 to 45 minutes or until deep golden brown and loaf sounds hollow when thumped. Using an instant-read thermometer, measure temperature in middle of one loaf. It should read 190°F or higher.

Remove loaves from pans by loosening around the sides and lifting from the bottom. Cool on wire cooling rack. You must allow loaves to cool about 30 minutes before slicing.

BAKER'S NOTES: When you begin to bake bread, it is best to use a thermometer to measure the temperature of the liquid before adding it to the yeast. I also like to use a thermometer to determine doneness. I have an instant-read thermometer that I use all the time.

Create a warm place for the dough to rise. Check and see if the top of your oven is warm. Or create a warm place by positioning a wire rack over a pan of hot water; change the water as it cools.

SECRETS TO SUCCESS: Two teaspoons of salt seems like a lot, but in addition to adding flavor, the salt also affects the yeast activity and conditions the dough.

HONEY WHEAT LOAF

Because the bran in wheat flour cuts the strands of the gluten, your bread will be heavy unless the dough also contains all-purpose or bread flour. In addition to sweetness, honey helps the bread stay fresher longer. Because of the lack of preservatives in homemade bread, it is usually best eaten within a day or two of baking or frozen to maintain freshness.

MAKES 1 LOAF

¾ cup warm water (105–115°F)
1 (¼-ounce) package active dry yeast
¾ cup warm milk
¼ cup butter
¼ cup honey
1 teaspoon salt
2½–3 cups bread flour, divided
2 cups whole-wheat flour

Sprinkle yeast over the warm water in bowl of a heavy-duty mixer and let stand 5 minutes. Heat milk in small saucepan over medium heat until it is 105 to 115°F. Remove pan from the heat and add butter, honey, and salt. Stir well to be sure the salt is dissolved. The butter doesn't have to melt.

Add milk mixture to the yeast. Add 1½ cups bread flour and all the wheat flour and beat on Medium speed 3 minutes. By hand, stir in enough additional bread flour to make a soft dough.

Place dough on a well-floured surface and shape it roughly into a ball. Place your fingers on top, curled slightly over the ball, and pull the dough toward you. Then push dough away, using the palms of your hands. Turn dough ¼ turn and repeat.

When you begin kneading, the dough will be sticky. Add bread flour a little at a time. As you knead, keep your fingers together and use the palms of your hands. Knead dough 6 to 8 minutes until it is smooth and elastic. You should not use more than 3 cups of bread flour, total.

Shape dough into a ball by pulling sides underneath to form a smooth top. Place it, top side down, in an oiled bowl. Turn the dough right side up, thus coating it with a little oil. Cover loosely with plastic wrap.

Let dough rise in a warm place until it doubles in size, about 1 hour. When it has doubled in size, the imprint will remain when you poke two fingers into the dough.

Grease bottom and part way up sides of 9 x 5-inch loaf pan.

Punch dough down, and place it on a lightly floured surface.

Roll dough out to an 8 x 14-inch rectangle. If it becomes difficult to shape, cover and let dough rest 5 to 10 minutes to relax the gluten. Roll dough up from short side and pinch edges to seal. Place dough in greased pan, seam side down. Loosely cover the pan with plastic wrap.

Let dough rise again 45 minutes or until doubled. Test by pressing dough lightly. If your finger leaves only a slight imprint the dough is ready.

Heat oven to 375°F with oven rack in lower third.

Bake 35 to 45 minutes or until deep golden brown and loaf sounds hollow when thumped. Using an instant-read thermometer, measure temperature in center of loaf. It should read 190 to 205°F.

Remove loaf from pan by loosening around sides and lifting from the bottom. Cool on wire cooling rack. You must let loaf cool slightly before slicing.

BAKER'S NOTE: Try using an electric knife to slice the loaf. If you slice it too soon, the dough will collapse and be mushy.

SECRETS TO SUCCESS: Whole-wheat flour should be stored in the freezer because the wheat germ can become rancid.

cinnamon swirl raisin Bread

Cinnamon sugar is swirled through this tender loaf as it is shaped. After the first rising, the raisins are kneaded into the dough. I love this bread warm from the oven, but after a day or two, it toasts beautifully. My method, which mixes the dry ingredients, including the yeast, before adding the warm liquid, saves preparation time.

MAKES 1 LOAF

3–3 ¼ cups bread or all-purpose flour, divided
¼ cup sugar
1 (¼-ounce) package active dry yeast
1 teaspoon salt
½ cup water
½ cup milk
¼ cup solid vegetable shortening
1 egg
¾ cup raisins

FILLING

2 tablespoons butter, melted
¾ cup sugar
1 teaspoon cinnamon

Place 1 cup flour, sugar, yeast, and salt in bowl of a heavy-duty mixer.

Heat water, milk and shortening in small saucepan to 120 to 130°F (it will feel hot on your wrist). Add mixture to mixer bowl and beat on Medium speed 2 minutes. Beat in egg. Stir in enough additional flour to make a soft dough.

To knead by hand, place dough on a well-floured surface and shape it roughly into a ball. Place your fingers on top, curled slightly over the ball, and pull the dough toward you. Then push dough away, using the palms of your hands. Turn dough ¼ turn and repeat.

When you begin kneading, the dough will be sticky. Add flour a little at a time. As you knead, keep your fingers together and use the palms of your hands. Knead dough 8 to 10 minutes until it is smooth and elastic. You should not use more than 3 ¼ cups of flour, total.

To judge whether the dough has been sufficiently kneaded, place it on the work surface, pull both ends gently, and release. The dough should be elastic and spring back. The dough should also be smooth and have little blisters of air that you can see under the surface.

Shape dough into a ball by pulling sides underneath to form a smooth top. Place it, top side down, in an oiled bowl. Turn the dough right side up, thus coating it with a little oil. Cover loosely with plastic wrap.

Let dough rise in a warm place for about 1 hour or until doubled. When it has doubled in size, the imprint will remain when you poke two fingers into it. Punch dough down and place it on a lightly floured surface. Knead in the raisins. Cover and let dough rest a few minutes to relax the gluten.

FILLING

Grease a 9 x 5-inch loaf pan. Roll the dough to a 16 x 8-inch rectangle. Brush with melted butter. Combine the sugar and cinnamon and sprinkle over dough. Starting with the short end roll the dough up tightly. (If dough isn't rolled tightly there will be a hole in the middle of the bread.) Pinch ends and seam and place seam side down in the pan.

Let dough rise again for about 30 minutes or until doubled. Test by pressing dough lightly. If your finger leaves only a slight imprint the dough is ready.

Heat oven to 375°F with oven rack in lower third. Bake 35 to 45 minutes or until deep golden brown and loaf sounds hollow when thumped. Using an instant-read thermometer, measure temperature in center of loaf. It should read 190°F or higher.

Remove loaf from pan by loosening around sides and lifting from the bottom. Cool on wire cooling rack. You must let loaf cool slightly before slicing.

BAKER'S NOTES: Because the yeast is mixed with the flour before the liquid is added, the liquid can be heated to a higher temperature. This method helps the dough rise faster.

Try using dried cranberries instead of raisins. They add a touch of crimson and a tangy sweetness.

SECRETS TO SUCCESS: Roll the dough tightly to avoid a hole in the middle of the loaf.

MULTI-GRAIN BREAD

This hearty bread has a chewy crumb and a yeasty flavor and is easy to make. After the first rise, the dough is shaped into a rustic country-style round loaf. For tender bread, always save some flour to add during kneading because the dough becomes less sticky as it's kneaded. Because this makes a large loaf, I first cut it into quarters and then into slices about ½ inch thick.

MAKES 1 LOAF

 1 cup water
½ cup milk
½ cup old-fashioned oats
½ cup firmly packed brown sugar
½ cup butter
1½ teaspoons salt
 1 (¼-ounce) package active dry yeast
¼ cup warm water (105–115°F)

3 ½–4 cups all-purpose flour, divided
1 cup whole wheat flour
½ cup sunflower nuts
1 egg, beaten
2 teaspoons water

Heat milk and 1 cup water in small saucepan over medium heat until very warm (120 to 130°F). Remove pan from heat and add oats, brown sugar, butter, and salt. Let mixture cool to lukewarm. The butter doesn't have to melt completely.

Sprinkle yeast over ¼ cup warm water to dissolve, and let stand about 5 minutes.

Place 1 cup all-purpose flour and 1 cup whole wheat flour in bowl of a heavy-duty mixer and stir to mix. Add oat mixture and yeast mixture to mixer bowl, and beat on Medium speed until well mixed. Scrape down sides of bowl and continue to beat 1 minute. Beat in 2 cups of remaining all-purpose flour. Stir in enough additional flour to form a soft dough. Stir in sunflower nuts.

To knead by hand, place dough on a well-floured surface and shape it roughly into a ball. Place your fingers on top, curled slightly over the ball, and pull the dough toward you. Then push dough away, using the palms of your hands. Turn dough ¼ turn and repeat.

When you begin kneading, this dough will be very sticky because of the whole wheat flour. Add flour a little at a time. As you knead, keep your fingers together and use the palms of your hands. Knead dough 8 to 10 minutes until it is smooth and elastic. You should not use more than 4 cups all-purpose flour, total.

To judge whether dough has been sufficiently kneaded, place it on work surface, pull both ends gently, and release. The dough should be elastic and spring back. The dough should also be smooth and have little blisters of air that you can see under the surface.

Shape dough into a ball by pulling sides underneath to form a smooth top. Place it, top side down, in an oiled bowl. Turn the dough right side up, thus coating it with a little oil. Cover loosely with plastic wrap.

Let dough rise in a warm place until it doubles in size, about 1 hour. When it has doubled, the imprint will remain when you poke two fingers into the dough. Punch down and place on a lightly floured surface.

Shape dough into a 9-inch smooth ball. An easy way to shape the ball is to pull sides to the bottom and smooth as you shape. Place dough on a greased baking sheet and press slightly to flatten. Cover and let rise in a warm place about 30 minutes or until doubled. Test by pressing dough lightly. A gentle touch should only leave a slight imprint.

Heat oven to 350°F with oven rack in lower third.

Combine egg and water and beat until smooth. Brush the egg wash over top and sides of loaf. Using a sharp knife, cut an "X" into the top of the dough.

Bake 50 to 60 minutes or until deep golden brown and loaf sounds hollow when thumped. Using an instant-read thermometer, measure temperature in center of loaf. It should read 190°F or higher. Cool bread on a wire cooling rack.

> BAKER'S NOTE: Place a silicone mat or piece of parchment paper on the cookie sheet when you use an egg wash. It will prevent the egg from burning onto the pan.

CHEWY OAT BUNS

Old-fashioned oats take longer to cook than quick cooking oats because they are cut into larger pieces, giving them a chewier texture. I use the old-fashioned oats for these dinner rolls, but quick cooking oats can also be used. I've made this recipe many times for Thanksgiving because it makes 24 buns. If there are any buns leftover, I just freeze them.

MAKES 24 BUNS

1 cup old-fashioned oats
2 cups boiling water
¼ cup firmly packed brown sugar
½ cup honey
2 tablespoons solid vegetable shortening
1 teaspoon salt
2 (¼-ounce) packages active dry yeast
½ cup warm water (105–115°F)
6–7 cups all-purpose flour

Combine oats and boiling water in large bowl. Stir in brown sugar, honey, shortening, and salt and cool to lukewarm.

Sprinkle yeast over the ½ cup warm water in small bowl and let stand 5 minutes. Stir yeast mixture into the warm oats mixture. Stir in enough flour to make a soft dough.

Place dough on well-floured surface and shape it roughly into a ball. Place your fingers, curled slightly, over the ball and pull dough toward you; then push dough away, using the palms of your hands. Turn dough ¼ turn and repeat, adding flour a little at a time. You should not use more than 7 cups flour, total.

Knead dough 8 to 10 minutes until it is smooth and elastic. To judge whether dough has been sufficiently kneaded, place it on work surface, pull both ends gently, and release. Dough should be elastic and spring back. Dough should also be smooth and have little blisters of air that you can see under the surface.

Shape dough into a ball by pulling sides underneath to form a smooth top. Place it, top side down, in an oiled bowl. Turn the dough right side up, thus coating it with a little oil. Cover loosely with plastic wrap.

Let dough rise in a warm place about 1 hour or until it doubles in size. When it has doubled in size, the imprint will remain when you poke two fingers into it. Punch down and place on lightly floured surface.

Grease a 15 x 10-inch jellyroll pan.

Divide dough into 24 pieces and shape into balls. Place balls on prepared pan. Cover and let rise about 30 minutes or until doubled. Test by pressing dough lightly. A gentle touch should only leave a slight imprint.

Heat oven to 350°F with oven rack in lower third. Bake 20 to 25 minutes or until golden brown. Bun bottoms should be browned.

> BAKER'S NOTES: As with any recipe containing yeast, the temperature of the liquids is very important. "Lukewarm" feels warm on the inside of your wrist.
>
> To speed cooling, place the bowl with the hot oats in a larger container filled with cold water.
>
> SECRETS TO SUCCESS: To shape the buns, roll them into rough balls, then pull down the sides to the bottom, smoothing the top. Place smooth side up on the baking pan.

CINNAMON TWISTS

Bake these cinnamon-flavored twists for your next brunch. The cinnamon–sugar coating gives them a sweet, crackled crust. They can be baked one day ahead and served at room temperature.

MAKES 24 TWISTS

½ cup milk
¼ cup water
¼ cup butter, cut-up
3 ¼–3 ¾ cups all-purpose flour, divided
¾ cup sugar, divided
½ teaspoon salt
1 (¼-ounce) package active dry yeast

1 egg
1 teaspoon cinnamon
⅓ cup butter, melted

Heat milk and water to 120 to 130°F in small saucepan over medium heat. Add butter.

Combine 1½ cups flour, ¼ cup sugar, salt, and yeast in bowl of a heavy-duty mixer. Add milk mixture to bowl and beat on Medium speed until well mixed.

Scrape down sides of bowl and beat 2 minutes. Beat in egg. Gradually add remaining flour and mix until soft dough forms.

Place dough on well-floured surface and shape it into a rough ball. Place your fingers curled slightly over ball and pull dough toward you; then push it away, using palms of your hands. Turn dough ¼ turn and repeat. Add flour a little at a time.

Knead dough 6 to 8 minutes until it is smooth and elastic. You should not use more than 3¾ cups of flour, total.

To judge whether dough has been sufficiently kneaded, place it on work surface, pull both ends gently, and release. Dough should be elastic and spring back. Dough also should be smooth and have little blisters of air that you can see under the surface.

Shape dough into a ball by pulling sides underneath to form a smooth top. Place it, top side down, in an oiled bowl. Turn the dough right side up, thus coating it with a little oil. Cover loosely with plastic wrap.

Let dough rise in a warm place for 1 hour or until doubled. When it has doubled in size, the imprint will remain when you poke two fingers into it.

Combine remaining sugar and cinnamon on one plate and place butter on another. Grease two cookie sheets generously with shortening.

Punch dough down and place it on lightly floured surface. Roll dough out to 12 x 12 inches. Cut into 12, 1-inch-long strips; cut each strip in half, forming 24, 6-inch-long strips. Dip each strip into the butter and then roll in the cinnamon-sugar. Twist each strip several times and place on cookie sheet.

Cover cookie sheets loosely and let twists rise for about 30 minutes or until doubled in size. Test by pressing dough lightly. A gentle touch should only leave a slight imprint.

Heat oven to 375°F with oven rack in middle. Bake 14 to 18 minutes or until golden brown. Cool on wire cooling racks.

BAKER'S NOTES: For easier clean-up, I use a silicone baking mat or parchment paper to line the baking sheets for this recipe

SECRETS TO SUCCESS: As I place each twist on the cookie sheet, I press both ends onto the sheet to keep the twist from untwisting.

caramel sticky buns

Although it takes time to make these buns, they are absolutely the best home-made caramel rolls I've ever eaten. The whipping cream in the caramel topping makes it silky smooth and rich. Add 1 cup of pecans to the pan if you prefer pecan rolls. Make the buns and refrigerate them overnight, then simply bake the next day.

MAKES 20 BUNS

1 cup milk
¼ cup water
½ cup butter, softened
4¾–5¼ cups all-purpose flour, divided
⅓ cup sugar
1 (¼-ounce) package active dry yeast
1 teaspoon salt
1 egg, beaten

TOPPING

> 1 ½ cups firmly packed brown sugar
> ½ cup butter, melted
> ⅓ cup whipping cream

FILLING

> 2 tablespoons butter, melted
> 1 cup firmly packed brown sugar
> 1 teaspoon cinnamon

Heat milk and water to 120 to 130°F. Add butter; it will not melt completely.

Place 2 cups flour, sugar, yeast, and salt in bowl of a heavy-duty mixer. Add milk mixture and beat on Medium speed until mixed. Scrape down sides of bowl and beat 3 minutes. Beat in egg and add enough flour to make soft dough.

Place dough on well-floured surface and shape it into a rough ball. Place your fingers, curled slightly, over ball and pull dough toward you; then push dough away, using palms of your hands. Turn dough ¼ turn and repeat.

When you begin kneading, dough will be sticky. Add flour a little at a time. As you knead, keep fingers together and use palms of your hands. Knead dough 6 to 8 minutes until it is smooth and elastic. You should not use more than 5 ¼ cups flour, total.

To judge whether dough has been sufficiently kneaded, place it on work surface, pull both ends gently, and release. Dough should be elastic and spring back. Little blisters of air should be visible just under the surface.

Shape dough into a ball by pulling sides underneath to form a smooth top. Place it, top side down, in an oiled bowl. Turn the dough right side up, thus coating it with a little oil. Cover loosely with plastic wrap.

Let dough rise in a warm place 1 hour or until it doubles. When it has doubled, the imprint will remain when you poke two fingers into dough. Punch dough down and place it on a lightly floured surface.

TOPPING

Combine topping ingredients in small bowl and mix well. Spread into a 13 x 9-inch baking pan.

FILLING

Roll out dough to 18 x 9-inch rectangle. Spread evenly with melted butter and sprinkle with brown sugar and cinnamon. Roll up, starting with long edge, and pinch edges to seal.

Cut into 20 slices (about ¾ inch thick). Place buns over topping in pan. Loosely cover pan with plastic wrap and let buns rise in a warm place 30 to 40 minutes or until doubled. Test by pressing dough lightly. A gentle touch should leave no imprint.

Heat oven to 350°F with oven rack in middle. Bake 35 to 40 minutes or until buns are golden brown and topping is bubbling up around them. Remove from oven.

Immediately, place a large pan or heatproof dish over the buns and quickly invert. Wait 1 minute before removing the baking pan. You can spread any topping left in the baking pan over the buns. Serve warm.

> BAKER'S NOTE: Before baking and after the buns are placed over the topping, they can be refrigerated overnight. Cover tightly. To bake, remove them from the refrigerator and let them stand at room temperature while the oven is heating.
>
> SECRETS TO SUCCESS: I usually turn the baked buns out onto a 15 x 10-baking pan. The pan or dish must be heatproof because the caramel is very hot and plastic breaks—I know!

ICE BOX ROLLS

Before the invention of refrigerators, home cooks used an "ice box" that was kept cold with a large piece of ice. Obviously, refrigerators are more reliable, but these breads kept their name of Ice Box Rolls. While the rolls are refrigerated overnight, the dough rises slowly. I prefer the cloverleaf rolls, but try all of the variations of these tender, buttery rolls and find your favorite.

MAKES 36 ROLLS

> 1 (¼-ounce) package active dry yeast
> ¼ cup warm water (105–115°F)
> 2 cups milk
> ½ cup sugar
> ⅓ cup butter, cut-up
> 1 teaspoon salt
> 6½–7 cups all-purpose flour, divided
> 1 egg, beaten

Sprinkle yeast over warm water in bowl of a heavy-duty mixer and let stand for 5 minutes.

Heat milk to very warm in small saucepan and add sugar, butter, and salt. Cool slightly.

Add milk mixture to yeast and stir in 3 cups flour. Beat on Medium speed until mixed. Scrape down sides of bowl and beat 3 minutes longer. Add egg and beat until mixed.

Beat in enough additional flour to form a soft, sticky dough. I save about ½ cup flour to use when shaping the dough. Cover and refrigerate overnight.

Scrape dough onto a lightly floured surface and punch down several times. Divide dough into thirds. Use a little flour to prevent sticking. Shape rolls as directed below.

Crescent Rolls. Lightly grease cookie sheet. Shape one-third of dough into a ball and roll out to a 10-inch circle. Cut into 12 wedges. Roll up each wedge, starting at wide end and rolling to the point. Place rolls point down as you place them on baking sheet. Cover loosely and let rise 45 minutes or until doubled. (Makes 12 rolls)

Cloverleaf Rolls. Lightly grease 12 cups in standard muffin pan. Place one-third of dough on floured surface and divide into 12 balls. To form cloverleaf rolls, further divide each ball into 3 pieces. Roll each piece into a ball, pulling the edges underneath to form a smooth top. Place 3 balls in each muffin cup. Cover loosely and let rise 45 minutes or until doubled. (Makes 12 rolls)

Round Dinner Rolls. Lightly grease a cookie sheet. Place one-third of dough on floured surface and divide into 12 pieces. Shape each piece into a ball about 2 inches in diameter; smooth the tops by pulling the sides to the bottom. Place on cookie sheet. Cover loosely and let rise 45 minutes or until doubled. (Makes 12 rolls)

TO BAKE THE ROLLS:

After the second rise, test rolls by pressing dough lightly. A gentle touch should leave no imprint.

Heat oven to 375°F with oven rack in middle. Bake 18 to 22 minutes or until rolls are golden brown. Serve warm or at room temperature.

SECRETS TO SUCCESS: I don't refrigerate the dough more than 24 hours because I think the flavor changes. After baking the rolls, I wrap them well and freeze them for later. Let thaw to room temperature before reheating. To reheat, place rolls in a 350°F oven for 6 to 10 minutes.

To make these rolls the same day, refrigerate the dough 4 hours. Continue with the recipe to shape and bake.

RAISIN FOCACCIA

I was sitting at a sidewalk café outside an Italian bakery in the North Beach area of San Francisco the first time I had raisin focaccia. Focaccia was the only thing sold at the bakery—but there were many choices including pizza, mushroom, olive, and rosemary. Focaccia is easy to make because it requires no kneading. Three rises create the chewy texture.

MAKES 8 TO 12 SERVINGS

> 2¾ cups all-purpose flour
> 1 tablespoon sugar
> 1 (¼-ounce) package active dry yeast
> ½ teaspoon salt
> 1 cup warm water (105–115°F)
> ¼ cup olive oil, divided
> ½ cup raisins

Combine flour, sugar, yeast, and salt in large bowl. Stir briefly to mix. Add water and 2 tablespoons olive oil and mix until a sticky batter is formed.

Cover bowl and let rise in a warm place 30 minutes. Dough will have risen but may not be doubled. Punch dough down, forcing out any large air bubbles. Allow dough to rise again for 30 minutes.

Spread 1 tablespoon olive oil in bottom of a 13 x 9-inch baking pan. Punch dough down and add raisins. You may need to add a little more flour at this point if dough is too sticky to handle.

Press dough into pan. Don't worry if it is irregular in shape. Just press it out as much as you can. Cover and let rise another 30 minutes.

Heat oven to 425°F with oven rack in lower third. Use the rounded handle of a wooden spoon (or your knuckles) to make indentations in the dough. Drizzle with remaining olive oil. Sprinkle with sugar if desired.

Bake 18 to 22 minutes or until golden brown on top and browned on bottom.

> BAKER'S NOTE: Lightly oil your hands if the dough is too sticky to handle.

onion, fig, and asiago focaccia

A traditional Italian focaccia is sprinkled with herbs, usually rosemary, and drizzled with olive oil, making it a nice addition to an Italian dinner. I also like to serve it cut into small wedges or squares as an appetizer. Unlike pizza, focaccia is served at room temperature. This is my son-in-law's favorite because it's easy to make and the contrast between the sweet figs and the caramelized onion is outstanding.

MAKES 8 TO 12 SERVINGS

2¾ cups all-purpose flour
1 tablespoon sugar
1 (¼-ounce) package active dry yeast
½ teaspoon coarse salt
1 cup very warm water (120–130°F)
¼ cup olive oil, divided
1 cup sliced onion (1 medium)
1 cup grated Asiago cheese
8 dried figs, coarsely chopped
2 teaspoons coarsely chopped fresh rosemary leaves
Coarse salt

Combine flour, sugar, yeast, and salt in large bowl. Add water and 2 tablespoons olive oil and mix until a sticky batter is formed.

Cover bowl and let batter rise in a warm place for 30 minutes. Dough will have risen but may not be doubled. Punch down, forcing out any large air bubbles. Cover loosely and allow dough to rise 15 minutes.

While dough is rising, heat remaining olive oil in a 9-inch skillet over medium heat. Add sliced onions and cook until tender. You will need to stir occasionally so onions don't burn. When cooked through, onions will be transparent. Cool slightly before placing onions on the dough. They will brown during baking.

Lightly spray a 12-inch pizza pan with nonstick cooking spray. Press dough in pan, pressing so it sticks to pan sides. Use handle of a wooden spoon or your knuckles to press dimples in the dough. Place onion slices on top, and sprinkle with cheese, figs, rosemary, and coarse salt. The oil from the onions will fill the dimples. Cover loosely and let rise 30 minutes.

Heat oven to 425°F with rack in lower third. Bake 20 to 25 minutes or until focaccia edges are brown and cheese is melted. Cool to room temperature and cut into wedges before serving.

BAKER'S NOTE: Remove the stems of the dried figs before chopping them.

SECRETS TO SUCCESS: If the crust begins to brown too quickly, place a second pizza sheet under the first. This creates an insulated pan so the focaccia bakes more slowly.

Fresh rosemary adds a woodsy flavor that I like. If fresh rosemary isn't available, use fresh thyme.

mini chocolate babkas

The word "babka" refers to a grandmother in Eastern Europe, and the shape of these rolls mimics her wide skirt. I've seen many interpretations of this bread, and I like these mini-rolls because they are a quick and easy adaptation. I've used hot roll mix to illustrate the fact that you can apply the same techniques without starting from scratch.

MAKES 36 BABKAS

> 1 (16-ounce) package hot roll mix
>
> 4 tablespoons sugar, divided
>
> 1 cup very warm water (120–130°F)
>
> 2 tablespoons soft butter
>
> 1 egg
>
> 1 tablespoon unsweetened cocoa
>
> 2 tablespoons butter, melted, divided
>
> 1 cup chocolate mini chips, divided

Prepare hot roll mix as directed on package. Add 2 tablespoons sugar to the dry ingredients before adding water, butter and egg. Knead dough 5 minutes or until smooth and elastic. Cover dough and let it rest for 5 minutes. Spray 36 cups in mini-muffin pans with nonstick cooking spray.

Combine 2 tablespoons sugar with unsweetened cocoa.

Divide dough in half and place one portion on lightly floured surface. Roll out dough to a rectangle about 15 x 9-inches and lightly brush with half of the melted butter. Sprinkle lightly with half of the cocoa mixture. Sprinkle with ½ cup mini chips. Starting at the long edge, roll up dough, enclosing filling. Pinch to seal. Cut into ¾-inch slices and place in prepared muffin cups. You should have 18 rolls. Repeat with remaining dough. Cover muffin pans and let dough rise about 30 minutes.

Heat oven to 375°F with oven rack in middle. Bake 15 to 18 minutes or until babkas are golden brown. Cool 5 minutes before removing rolls from muffin cups. Dust generously with powdered sugar or drizzle with Powdered Sugar Glaze (see page 283).

> BAKER'S NOTES: If you don't have 3 mini-muffin pans, shape one log and chill the other log until it's needed. It won't rise in the refrigerator and can be used when the pan is available.
>
> Cover the pans loosely with plastic wrap for rising. If you spray the plastic wrap with nonstick cooking spray it won't stick to rolls.

Basic Pizza

Homemade crust makes "pizza night' an occasion the whole family will look forward to. Spread the sauce on the pre-baked crust and let everyone choose his or her own toppings. When I only need one pizza, I pre-bake the second crust and freeze it. With a crust from the freezer, homemade pizza arrives faster than delivery!

MAKES 2 (12-inch) PIZZAS

Basic Pizza Crust

1 (¼-ounce) package active dry yeast
1 cup warm water (105–115°F)
3 cups all-purpose flour, divided
1 tablespoon sugar
½ teaspoon salt
1 tablespoon olive oil

TOPPING

>
> 1 (15-ounce) can pizza sauce
>
> 2–3 cups shredded mozzarella cheese
>
> Pizza toppings: cooked Italian sausage, chopped green peppers, sliced mushrooms, olives, etc.

BASIC PIZZA CRUST

Sprinkle yeast over warm water in small bowl and let stand about 5 minutes. Combine 2½ cups flour, sugar, and salt in large bowl. Stir in yeast mixture and olive oil. Continue stirring until flour is absorbed. Stir in remaining flour until a soft dough is formed. Dough will be sticky to start with, but after kneading it becomes easier to handle.

Place dough on well-floured surface and shape it into a ball. Place your fingers on top of dough ball, curled slightly, and pull dough toward you; then push it away, using palms of your hands. Turn dough ¼ turn and repeat. Knead dough 6 to 8 minutes or until it is smooth and elastic.

To judge whether dough has been sufficiently kneaded, place it on work surface, pull both ends gently, and release. Dough should be elastic and spring back. Little blisters of air should be visible just under the surface.

If dough is sticky, gradually add flour while kneading. Do not use more than 3 cups flour, total. Shape dough into a ball by pulling sides underneath forming a smooth top. Cover dough and let it rest while you prepare toppings. I just invert a bowl over the dough for this short rest.

Heat oven to 450°F. For crispest crust, place rack toward bottom of oven.

Grease two 12-inch pizza pans. Leave about 1 inch around edge of each pan ungreased so dough has something to cling to as it is stretched to fill pan. Place half of dough in center of each pan, and push it out to pan edges, rotating pan as you go. Form a raised edge around the crust's perimeter.

Bake crusts 7 to 10 minutes or until they are just beginning to brown. Remove from oven. (The crusts can be frozen at this point. Cool to room temperature and wrap tightly before freezing.)

TOPPING

Spread 1 cup pizza sauce over each crust and add toppings. Sprinkle 1 to 1 ½ cups shredded mozzarella cheese over each pizza. Bake 7 to 10 minutes longer until cheese is melted and crust is browned. Cool slightly before cutting.

calzones

A calzone is a stuffed pizza. Everyone can have their own piece of dough and fill it as they like. This is a great recipe for nights when the family cooks together. Start with homemade pizza dough, and let everyone prepare his or her own calzone. You may use any toppings you like—just don't fill the dough too full. I like to serve the calzones with extra sauce for dipping.

MAKES 4 CALZONES

> 1 tablespoon cornmeal
> Basic Pizza Crust (see page 271)
> 1 (15-ounce) can pizza sauce
> 1 cup shredded mozzarella cheese

EXTRAS:

> Pepperoni slices
> Italian sausage, cooked and crumbled
> Fresh sliced mushrooms
> Chopped green pepper
> Sliced ripe olives

Heat oven to 400°F with rack in lower third. Spray a baking sheet with nonstick cooking spray and sprinkle with cornmeal.

Lightly flour working surface. Divide pizza dough into 4 parts. Roll each part into an 8-inch circle. Spread ¼ cup pizza sauce over half of each circle. Sprinkle ¼ cup cheese over sauce. You can add about ½ cup additional "extras" to each calzone. Fold circles in half. Press edges together and pinch to seal. After I pinch the edges, I roll them and press again. Place on baking sheet and cut several slits into top of each calzone.

Bake about 18 minutes or until golden brown. Cool slightly before serving.

STROMBOLI

Stromboli is another family favorite, and that's why I've included this recipe. I don't put pizza sauce inside so the meat and cheese flavors will predominate. I've served this for dinner, but it makes a popular snack when everyone is gathered for the big game. You can use various deli meats and cheeses and add olives or hot peppers—just don't fill the stromboli too full. Provolone, a mild Italian cheese with a smoky flavor, is perfect here.

MAKES 12 TO 15 SERVINGS

> Basic pizza crust (see page 271)
> 1 tablespoon olive oil
> ¼ pound sliced pepperoni
> ¼ pound sliced hard salami
> 4 ounces Provolone cheese, sliced or shredded
> 1 egg, beaten
> Grated Parmesan cheese

Heat oven to 400°F with rack in lower third. Lightly grease a cookie sheet.

Place dough on lightly floured surface and roll out to a 15 x 12-inch rectangle. If dough becomes difficult to roll, let is rest briefly.

Brush dough with olive oil. Arrange pepperoni, salami, and Provolone cheese down center of dough. Fold both sides toward the center and pinch together to seal. Brush egg over top of dough. Sprinkle with Parmesan cheese and place on prepared cookie sheet. The easiest way to lift the dough is with large metal spatulas at each end. Cut several slits into dough.

Beat 30 to 35 minutes or until stromboli are well browned. Cool slightly before slicing. Serve with pizza or marinara sauce for dipping.

> BAKER'S NOTE: Cover the baking sheet with a silicone baking mat for easy clean-up since leaks do occur.

DOUBLE-QUICK COFFEE CAKE

Fast-rising yeast is processed so that it is easily activated and works faster; only a short 10-minutes is needed for the first rise. After shaping the dough, it still needs to rise until it doubles in size, but the prep time is halved.

MAKES 8 SERVINGS

1 (¼-ounce) package fast-rising yeast
¼ cup warm water (105–115°F)
½ cup milk
¼ cup sugar
¼ cup butter
1 teaspoon salt
2¾–3 cups all-purpose flour, divided
1 egg, beaten

TOPPING

> 2 tablespoons butter, melted
> ¼ cup firmly packed brown sugar
> 1 teaspoon cinnamon

Sprinkle yeast over warm water in bowl of a heavy-duty mixer and let stand 5 minutes. Heat milk to lukewarm, or warm to the touch. Add sugar, butter, and salt. The butter doesn't need to be completely melted. Cool slightly.

Add milk mixture to yeast mixture and stir in 1½ cups flour. Beat on Medium-High speed until well combined. Beat in egg. Stir in additional flour to form a soft dough.

Place dough on well-floured surface and shape it into a ball. Place your fingers on top of dough ball, curled slightly, and pull dough toward you; then push it away, using palms of your hands. Turn dough ¼ turn and repeat. Knead until smooth and elastic, about 5 minutes.

To judge whether dough has been sufficiently kneaded, place it on work surface, pull both ends gently, and release. Dough should be elastic and spring back. Little blisters of air should be visible just under the surface.

Cover and let dough rest 10 minutes. I just invert a bowl over the dough.

Shape dough into a ball by pulling sides underneath forming a smooth top. Lightly grease a 9-inch round cake pan. Press dough into pan, pressing it into the sides of the pan to shape it. Cover and let rise in a warm place 30 to 45 minutes or until doubled.

TOPPING

Heat oven to 350°F with rack in middle. Brush dough with melted butter. Mix the brown sugar and cinnamon together and sprinkle over dough.

Bake 30 to 40 minutes or until golden brown. Cool in pan for 5 minutes before serving. Serve warm.

BAKER'S NOTE: You can also bake this coffee cake in a lightly greased 8 x 8-inch baking pan. Bake 30 to 35 minutes or until golden brown.

easy HERB DINNER ROLLS

Fast-rising yeast makes these rolls easy enough to make any time. I actually purchased herbes de Provence at a market in the South of France. It usually includes basil, marjoram, sage, thyme, rosemary, and lavender. You can use any combination of herbs you like.

MAKES 12 ROLLS

1 (¼-ounce) package fast-rising yeast
1 cup warm water (105–115°F)
1 tablespoon sugar
1 tablespoon solid vegetable shortening
2½–3 cups all-purpose flour, divided
1 teaspoon salt
1 teaspoon herbes de Provence
1 tablespoon butter, melted

Sprinkle yeast into warm water in bowl of a heavy-duty mixer. Add sugar and shortening and stir. Let stand 5 minutes. Add 1½ cups flour, salt, and herbes de Provence and beat until well mixed. Stir in enough remaining flour to make a soft dough. Save at least ¼ cup of flour to add while kneading the dough.

Place dough on well-floured surface and shape it into a ball. Place your fingers on top of dough ball, curled slightly, and pull dough toward you; then push it away, using palms of your hands. Turn dough ¼ turn and repeat. Knead until smooth and elastic, about 5 to 8 minutes.

To judge whether dough has been sufficiently kneaded, place it on work surface, pull both ends gently, and release. Dough should be elastic and spring back. Little blisters of air should be visible just under the surface.

Cover and let dough rest 10 minutes. I just invert a bowl over the dough.

Lightly grease a 13 x 9-inch baking pan. Punch dough down and divide it into 12 pieces. Shape dough into balls by pulling the sides underneath forming a smooth top. Place in prepared pan.

Cover pan and let dough rise in a warm place about 30 minutes or until rolls have doubled in volume. Test by pressing dough lightly. If your finger leaves only a slight imprint the dough is ready.

Heat oven to 400°F with rack in middle. Bake rolls 15 to 20 minutes or until they are golden brown. After rolls are removed from oven, brush them with melted butter.

SECRETS TO SUCCESS: To form the rolls, I divide the dough in half and then continue to divide each half until I have 12 pieces. If the pieces are very uneven, pinch dough from larger balls and add it to smaller balls so the rolls bake evenly.

chapter twelve

Beyond the Basics

THE RECIPES IN THIS CHAPTER include the embellishments that transform a cake from basic to deluxe or a fruit tart to extraordinary or a brownie to out-of-this-world. It's up to you whether to use a luscious Creamy Chocolate or elegant Buttercream Frosting when you assemble a layer cake, but the small extra effort is sure to evoke many compliments. Fill a tart with Pastry Cream and you will have a completely different result. Your muffins and cookies will take on a new dimension when you finish them off with Powdered Sugar Glaze. I've also included some fancy-but-easy garnishes such as chocolate heart cut-outs and strawberry fans to add to your Trifle. And remember, a simple dusting of powdered sugar is easy and quick.

BUTTERCREAM FROSTING

Use this frosting for cakes, bars, or cookies. I start with the minimum amount of milk because it is easier to beat the frosting until smooth when it is thick. If your powdered sugar is lumpy, sifting it will make a smoother frosting.

FROSTS A 2-LAYER OR 13 X 9-INCH CAKE

⅓ cup butter, melted
3 cups powdered sugar
1½ teaspoons vanilla
2–3 tablespoons milk

Combine butter, powdered sugar, vanilla, and 2 tablespoons milk in bowl of a heavy-duty mixer. Beat on Medium speed until smooth, scraping down sides of bowl occasionally. Dilute with milk until frosting is spreadable but firm enough to hold swirls.

CREAMY CHOCOLATE FROSTING

It seems like everyone's favorite flavor combination is yellow cake with chocolate frosting, and this recipe is loaded with chocolate flavor.

FROSTS A 2-LAYER OR 13 X 9-INCH CAKE

3½ cups powdered sugar
1 cup unsweetened cocoa
1 cup butter, softened
6–8 tablespoons milk
2 teaspoons vanilla

Combine powdered sugar, cocoa, butter, 6 tablespoons milk, and vanilla in bowl of a heavy-duty mixer. Beat on Medium speed until smooth, scraping down sides of bowl occasionally. Dilute with additional milk until frosting is spreadable but firm enough to hold swirls.

WHIPPED CREAM CHEESE FROSTING

This frosting has the slight tang that comes from cream cheese, but it's lighter than most cream cheese frostings. For the best results, the cream cheese must be at room temperature and the whipping cream should be cold. Be sure to refrigerate the frosted cake or the frosting will collapse.

FROSTS A 2-LAYER OR 13 X 9-INCH CAKE

> 1 (8-ounce) package cream cheese, softened
> 2 cups powdered sugar, sifted
> 1 teaspoon vanilla
> 1 cup whipping cream

Place cream cheese in bowl of a heavy-duty mixer and beat on Medium speed until creamy and smooth. Gradually add powdered sugar, vanilla, and whipping cream. Scrape down the sides of the bowl. Increase speed to High and beat until light and fluffy and soft enough to spread. After frosting cake, store in refrigerator.

CREAMY WHIPPED FROSTING

This is the frosting that always covered my birthday cakes when I was growing up. It is from Dudt's Bakery, a well-known old-fashioned bakery in Pittsburgh that has been closed for many years.

MAKES 3 CUPS

¾ cup butter, divided
¼ cup all-purpose flour
1 cup milk
½ cup solid vegetable shortening
1 cup sugar
1 teaspoon vanilla

Melt ¼ cup butter in small saucepan and stir in flour. Cook about 1 minute, stirring constantly. Add milk and stir with a whisk until sauce comes to a vigorous boil and thickens. Remove from heat and cover surface with plastic wrap to prevent skin from forming. Cool to room temperature.

Beat remaining ½ cup butter and shortening in bowl of a heavy-duty mixer until creamy. Add sugar and vanilla and beat 2 minutes. Gradually add the sauce and beat 2 minutes more or until light and creamy and sugar is dissolved.

CHOCOLATE GANACHE

Chocolate Ganache is a combination of whipping cream and chocolate that makes a smooth shiny glaze. Use the best quality chocolate you can find. Try making sandwich cookies with ganache as the filling.

MAKES 1 ½ CUPS

> 8 ounces semisweet chocolate, coarsely chopped
> ½ cup whipping cream

Melt chocolate with whipping cream in small saucepan over low heat, stirring occasionally. Whisk until smooth. Cool to the right consistency before using. If ganache gets too thick, heat it slightly. Don't refrigerate or it will lose its shine. Ganache takes a couple of hours to set.

POWDERED SUGAR GLAZE

Use this glaze on sweet rolls, muffins, and cookies to add a finishing touch or when a little more sweetness is needed. Sift the powdered sugar for a smooth glaze.

MAKES ½ CUP

> 1 cup powdered sugar
> ½ teaspoon vanilla
> 2–3 tablespoons whipping cream

Combine powdered sugar, vanilla, and 2 tablespoons whipping cream in small bowl. Beat until smooth. Add more whipping cream until glaze is thin enough to drizzle.

CUSTARD SAUCE

When making a custard sauce, it is essential not to cook the sauce too long after adding the eggs or it will curdle. I like this custard sauce because it contains cornstarch in addition to the egg yolks, so it is less likely to curdle. When I serve it with bread pudding, I stir in two tablespoons bourbon or whiskey.

MAKES 2 CUPS

> 1 ½ cups half-and-half
> ½ cup sugar
> 1 tablespoon cornstarch
> 4 egg yolks
> 1 teaspoon vanilla

Heat half-and-half in small saucepan until it almost comes to a boil. Mix sugar with cornstarch in small bowl.

Whisk the egg yolks in large bowl until well mixed. Add sugar mixture and continue whisking until the mixture lightens in color. Slowly stir in the hot half-and-half, beating constantly with a whisk.

Return mixture to saucepan and cook over low heat, whisking constantly until mixture thickens. Don't let sauce boil or it will curdle. (I use an instant-read thermometer and cook to 160°F).

Remove from heat and stir in vanilla. Press a piece of plastic wrap on the surface to prevent a film from forming.

PASTRY CREAM

Pastry cream is used in Trifle and as a filling for pies and tarts. The eggs are tempered (which means warmed slightly) before they are added to the hot milk mixture so that they don't curdle. Place a wet cloth under the bowl with the eggs, and it won't move while you are beating. Making pastry cream can be challenging but becomes easy with practice. And there's always vanilla pudding!

MAKES 3 CUPS

> ¾ cup sugar
> 3 tablespoons cornstarch
> ⅛ teaspoon salt
> 3 cups milk
> 2 eggs, well beaten
> 1 tablespoon butter
> 2 teaspoons vanilla

Place sugar, cornstarch, and salt in heavy saucepan. Slowly stir in milk, stirring until cornstarch dissolves. Cook over medium heat, stirring constantly, until sauce comes to a boil. Reduce heat to low and boil 1 minute, stirring constantly.

Remove pan from heat. Beat eggs in separate bowl. Slowly pour about 1 cup hot pudding into eggs, while beating constantly, until completely mixed.

Gradually pour the warmed eggs back into the hot pudding while whisking or stirring rapidly. Return pan to heat and cook on low, stirring constantly, about 1 minute or until mixture thickens. Do not let pudding boil or eggs will curdle. (I use an instant-read thermometer and cook to 160°F).

Stir in butter and vanilla. Remove from heat and press a piece of plastic wrap on surface of the pastry cream to prevent a skin from forming. Cool and store in the refrigerator.

new orleans praline sauce

New Orleans is famous for Pecan Pralines and this sauce captures those same flavors. If the rum isn't warm, it won't ignite; you can omit it if you like. Serve over ice cream, brownies, or pancakes.

MAKES 1 CUP

½ cup butter
1 cup firmly packed light brown sugar
¼ cup whipping cream
2 tablespoons dark rum, warmed
½ cup pecan pieces, toasted

Melt butter in small saucepan over medium heat. Add brown sugar and whipping cream and cook, stirring constantly, until mixture comes to a boil. Reduce heat to low and cook 1 minute. Remove pan from heat. Add warm rum (heat rum in small saucepan) and carefully ignite. The rum will flame up. Add pecans. Serve warm.

STRAWBERRY sauce

A drop or two of balsamic vinegar enhances the fresh strawberry flavor.
Use this sauce to make a perfect shortcake or ice cream sundae.

MAKES 2 CUPS

¼ cup water
2 tablespoons sugar
1 teaspoon cornstarch
½ teaspoon lemon juice
¼ teaspoon balsamic vinegar
½ teaspoon almond extract
2 cups sliced fresh strawberries

Place water, sugar, cornstarch, lemon juice and vinegar in small saucepan. Bring to a boil over medium heat. Cook about 1 minute, stirring constantly, until thickened and clear. Stir in almond extract. Pour over strawberries. Let stand at room temperature about ½ hour. Serve over shortcake, angel food cake or ice cream.

vanilla whipped cream

Don't use ultra-pasteurized whipping cream, and chill your bowl and beaters before whipping the cream for best results. A delicate flavor comes from the addition of a vanilla bean, but 1 teaspoon of vanilla extract is an everyday substitute.

MAKES ABOUT 2 1/2 CUPS

> 1 cup whipping cream
> 1/2 vanilla bean or 1 teaspoon vanilla
> 2 tablespoons powdered sugar

Place whipping cream in bowl of a heavy-duty mixer. Cut vanilla bean open lengthwise, exposing the seeds. With the tip of a knife, scrape seeds into the whipping cream.

Beat at High speed in bowl of a heavy-duty mixer fitted with the whisk until soft peaks form. Scrape down sides of bowl, and add powdered sugar. Beat until sugar is dissolved and stiff peaks form. Chill until serving.

hot fudge sauce

Hot fudge sauce can be used many ways in addition to topping ice cream— but that's probably the best. The unsweetened chocolate adds to the overall chocolate flavor.

MAKES 2 CUPS

4 ounces bittersweet or semisweet chocolate, chopped
1 ounce unsweetened chocolate, chopped
½ cup butter
2 cups powdered sugar
1 (12-ounce) can evaporated milk
Pinch of salt
1 teaspoon vanilla

Combine all ingredients, except vanilla, in heavy, medium-size saucepan. Cook over medium-low heat until mixture comes to a boil, stirring constantly. Reduce heat to low, and cook 4 to 5 minutes or until thickened, stirring occasionally. Remove from heat and stir in vanilla. Cool and store in refrigerator. Reheat to serve.

easy caramel sauce

I like this sauce almost as much as homemade caramels because it has the same buttery flavor. Serve it slightly warm with ice cream or a fruit dessert like apple crisp.

MAKES 1 ½ CUPS

1 cup firmly packed brown sugar
½ cup whipping cream
2 tablespoons corn syrup
¼ cup butter

Combine all ingredients in heavy, medium-size saucepan. Cook over medium-low heat until mixture comes to a boil, stirring constantly. Reduce heat to low, and cook 4 to 5 minutes or until thickened, stirring occasionally. Cool and store in refrigerator. Reheat to serve.

Lemon Curd

Try making your own Lemon Curd and then compare it to a jar you have purchased. The homemade flavor is a winner. Serve this with scones, fresh fruits, or use it as a tart or cake filling. Don't forget to grate the lemon peel before squeezing the juice.

MAKES 1 1/4 CUPS

> 1/2 cup sugar
> 1/2 cup freshly squeezed lemon juice
> 2 teaspoons grated lemon peel
> 1/4 cup butter
> 2 eggs, beaten

Combine all ingredients in heavy, small-size saucepan and cook over medium-low heat, stirring constantly. Bring mixture just to the point where some bubbles rise and sauce has thickened, 6 to 8 minutes. Use a silicone spatula for stirring, and cook until sauce coats the spatula. When you draw your finger across the back of the spatula, the path should remain. Strain into small bowl and cover with plastic wrap. Cool to room temperature and refrigerate.

Homemade Crème Fraîche

Crème fraîche is usually available at most supermarkets, but it is also easy to make your own. After it has thickened, it will keep about 3 weeks in the refrigerator. It is delicious in sauces or soups. Try it instead of whipped cream or ice cream on fruit desserts.

MAKES 1 1/4 CUPS

1 cup whipping cream
¼ cup lowfat buttermilk

Heat whipping cream in small saucepan until warm to the touch (100 to 110°F). Stir in buttermilk. Cover and let stand at room temperature about 24 hours. After crème fraîche has thickened, store it in refrigerator.

SIMPLE GARNISHES

Any one of the following garnishes make an everyday dessert something special. Don't forget a few raspberries and mint leaves provide a splash of color that is always appreciated.

Edible flowers are a dainty and colorful garnish. Buy them at farmer's markets or with the herbs in the supermarket. Ask to be sure they are safe to eat.

Tint vanilla frosting with food colors before spreading on cookies or cupcakes.

Coarse sugar or sanding sugar can be sprinkled on shortcakes, muffins or cookies before baking and will retain its shape.

STRAWBERRY FANS

Choose large, perfect berries for cutting into fans. Starting at the tip, slice toward the stem end, but do not cut all the way through. Make several cuts and open into a fan shape.

CHOCOLATE GARNISHES

Use high quality chocolate for your garnishes. It is better to use squares or pieces rather than chocolate morsels, which don't melt as well.

8 ounces semisweet chocolate, chopped

Melt chocolate in double boiler over, not in, simmering water until smooth. Pour melted chocolate onto a silicone baking mat or piece of parchment paper. Spread evenly. Cool until firm.

To make heart cut-outs, spread chocolate to about ⅜ inch thickness. When completely cool, cut out small hearts or other shapes and add to desserts.

Chocolate can also be spread in a thin layer, and after cooling, you can break off small pieces to place on top of desserts.

CHOCOLATE CURLS

Warm the edge of a semisweet chocolate bar with your hand. Pull a vegetable peeler along the edge forming curls. Use a toothpick to lift curls.

index